THE MASS: UNDERSTANDING WHAT'S WHAT

THE

MASS

UNDERSTANDING
WHAT'S WHAT

PATRICK MULLINS OCarm

VERITAS

First published 2009 by
Veritas Publications
7–8 Lower Abbey Street
Dublin 1
Ireland
Email publications@veritas.ie
Website www.veritas.ie

ISBN 978 1 84730 201 4

10 9 8 7 6 5 4 3 2 1

Designed by Colette Dower
Printed in the Republic of Ireland by ColourBooks Ltd, Dublin

Veritas books are printed on paper made from the wood pulp of
managed forests. For every tree felled, at least one tree is planted,
thereby renewing natural resources.

CONTENTS

INTRODUCTION

This book is a guide for those who want to understand the Mass better, to participate in it more fully and to make it the focus and nourishment of their lives.

The first chapter invites the reader to consider the significance of the Last Supper as a meal in the days leading up to Passover and, in that way, to understand the Old Testament origins of the Christian Eucharist. It also sketches the way in which the celebration of the Eucharist developed between the New Testament and the present.

The second chapter looks at the four parts of the Mass: the Preparatory Rites, the Liturgy of the Word, the Liturgy of the Eucharist and the Concluding Rites. It explores the role and function of each part in a way that invites those who participate to enter more fully and actively into the celebration of the Eucharist.

The third chapter describes the different roles and functions of both clergy and lay people when the Eucharist is celebrated. In addition to the celebrant and concelebrants, the Deacons, Acolytes, Lectors, Extraordinary Ministers of the Word, Extraordinary

Ministers of Holy Communion, and the musicians and singers all make an important contribution. The assembled congregation should also participate actively, rather than passively, in the sacramental action.

The fourth chapter outlines the physical arrangement of the church where Mass is celebrated, the different seasons of the liturgical year and the significance of the liturgical colours and postures.

Chapter five looks at some of the technical terms that are used in relation to the Mass (sacrifice, sacrament, transubstantiation and mystical Body). It also outlines the significance of these terms in the light of Catholic doctrine concerning the Eucharist.

The sixth chapter looks at the way we are changed and drawn into Christ's self-sacrificing love by the Mass and of the 'Eucharistic rhythm' it gives to our Christian way of life.

Each chapter includes a selection of books and websites for further reading and reflection. The abbreviation GIRM refers to the English translation for England and Wales (2005) of the *General Instruction of the Roman Missal*, issued in 2002. This text, in pdf format, may be downloaded from the Liturgy Office of England and Wales website: http://www.liturgyoffice.org.uk/Resources/GIRM/Documents/index.html.

CHAPTER 1
THE LAST SUPPER

One of the best ways to deepen our understanding of the Mass is to investigate how it first began at the Last Supper. In this chapter, we will begin by exploring the relationship between the Last Supper and the Jewish feast of Passover. We will see that the Christian Eucharist has its roots in the Old Testament. We will also outline the way in which the first Eucharist, the Last Supper, evolved over time into the Mass that is celebrated in our churches every weekend.

The Gospels and the Tradition
The four Gospels are our principal sources for the life and teaching of Jesus. We believe that they faithfully hand on to us what Jesus, the Son of God, really did and taught for our salvation. The Second Vatican Council (1962–65)[1] reminds us, however, that they are literary compositions based on earlier traditions.

> The sacred authors, in writing the four Gospels, selected certain of the many elements which had been handed on, either orally or already in written form;

---

1 See Vatican II's Dogmatic Constitution on Divine Revelation, *Dei verbum*, 19. This text is quoted in the *Catechism of the Catholic Church*, 126.

others they synthesized or explained with an eye to the situation of the churches, while sustaining the form of preaching, but always in such a fashion that they have told us the honest truth about Jesus.

Writing their Gospels many years after the events they were describing, each of the four Evangelists 'told us the honest truth about Jesus' in their own particular way, taking the situation of their intended readers into account. Although they retain the sense of what Jesus said and did, they do not always describe events in the same way. As we shall see, they sometimes differ from one another on particular points, such as the circumstances in which particular events took place. All four Gospels tell us that the Last Supper took place in Jerusalem during the annual pilgrimage feast of Passover. Mark, followed by Luke and Matthew, presents the Last Supper as taking place on the first day of Unleavened Bread. John, however, says that it took place two days earlier. At first sight, this discrepancy might give the impression that the Gospel accounts might be historically unreliable. As we shall see, however, they were inviting their readers to understand the meaning of the same event, the Last Supper, but in different ways.

The Last Supper and the Jewish Passover[2]
Among the Jews, the spring festival of Passover and Unleavened Bread, commemorating the Exodus of the Jews from Egypt and the first harvest when they returned to Israel, was celebrated in the middle of the first month of the Jewish year, known as Nisan. For the Jews, each

---

2 On Passover, see http://en.wikipedia.org/wiki/Passover.

day began, not with dawn, but with nightfall and it continued until the following nightfall. Chapter 23 of the Old Testament book of Leviticus laid down that the double feast of Passover and Unleavened Bread should begin on the evening of the fourteenth day of Nisan with the slaughter of the Passover lambs (usually in the afternoon).The Passover meal was celebrated that evening which, by their reckoning, was the beginning of Nisan, the first of the seven days of Unleavened Bread. During the seven days of the feast of Unleavened Bread, only bread made from fresh grain, without the addition of any yeast left over from the previous year, was to be eaten. Each day, an offering was made to the Lord by means of fire (see Lev 23:8).

The Gospel of Mark says that the Last Supper took place on the fifteenth day of Nisan, the first day of Unleavened Bread, when the Passover lamb was sacrificed and the Passover meal eaten:

> And on the first day of Unleavened Bread, when they sacrificed the Passover lamb, his disciples said to him, 'Where will you have us go and prepare for you to eat the Passover?' ... And the disciples set out and went to the city and found it as he had told them; and they prepared the Passover. (Mk 14:12, 16)

Like Mark, Matthew (see Mt 26:17-29) and Luke (see Lk 22:7-13) present the Last Supper as taking place on the first day of Unleavened Bread, the fifteenth day of Nisan, and the crucifixion as taking place the following day, the sixteenth day of Nisan. According to John 19:14, however, Jesus died on the cross on Passover Preparation Day, the fourteenth day of Nisan,[3] the day on which the Passover lambs were slaughtered, and the Last Supper took place the previous evening, the thirteenth day of Nisan. For John, in other words, the Last Supper was not, as such, a Passover meal (always celebrated on the fifteenth day of Nisan) but a pre-Passover meal celebrated two days earlier, on the thirteenth day of Nisan.

The behaviour of the chief priests and scribes on the night before Jesus died is difficult to reconcile with the dating in Matthew, Mark and Luke, since, as John 18:28 implies, it would probably have contradicted the requirement that people should abstain from their normal occupations during the week-long celebration of the feast of Unleavened Bread. Most commentators think that John's chronology is more likely to be correct and that Mark, followed by Matthew and Luke, presented the Last Supper as a Passover meal in order to associate the events leading up to Jesus' death with the great Passover themes of the sacrificial lamb and liberation from slavery. In either case, of course, the implication is that the Jewish feast of Passover and Unleavened Bread provided the key to understanding what happened at the Last Supper. In the next section, we explore how these Jewish feasts help us to understand the Eucharist.

The Celebration of the Jewish Passover and the Mass[4]
The Passover ('*Pesach*' in Hebrew) sacrifice could be performed only in Jerusalem (see Dt 16:2-6). Every year,

---

3 See Pheme Perkins, 'The Gospel According to John' in *The New Jerome Biblical Commentary*, Student Edition (London: Geoffrey Chapman, 1990) pp. 942–85 at 973.
4 See Jean-Marie R. Tillard, *The Eucharist Pasch of God's People* (New York: Alba, 1967).

many Jews came to the city on pilgrimage for its celebration. It marked a new beginning for the Israelites and any yeast made from fermenting the previous year's grain was disposed of before the feast began (see Ex 13:7). Four days before the feast, on the tenth day of Nisan, each household set apart a year-old, unblemished male lamb (or goat). The feast began with the slaughter of the lamb 'between the two evenings' (usually the afternoon) of the fourteenth Nisan. Some of the blood of the slaughtered lamb was put on the doorposts and lintel of the house in memory of the last of the ten plagues when 'God struck every firstborn' son among the Egyptians (see Ex 12:29) but spared the houses of the Israelites. The roasted lamb was eaten with unleavened bread (*matzoth*) and bitter herbs 'that night', i.e. the fifteenth Nisan. This particular meal, known as a *Seder*, began with a thanksgiving blessing over the wine, an account of the Exodus from Egypt and a thanksgiving blessing when the unleavened bread was broken and distributed by the head of the household.

When all had finished eating, there was a concluding blessing, the recitation of the psalms of praise and the final blessing over the wine. In the course of the meal, three cups of wine were passed around, the first during the blessing of the wine at the beginning of the meal, the second during the account of the Exodus and the third at the blessing when all had finished eating.[5] Whatever remained of the roasted lamb at sunrise was burned (see Ex 12:3-10). That day, the sixteenth Nisan, was known as

---

5 In a later period, a fourth cup of wine was passed around after the psalms of praise had been recited.

the first day of the Omer. The fiftieth day of the Omer was the feast of Pentecost (*Shavuot*), commemorating the covenant established between God and the people of Israel on Mount Sinai. On the eighth day of the Omer, the final day of Unleavened Bread, the crossing of the Red Sea by the people of Israel and the destruction of their enemies was commemorated with special prayer services and another festive meal.

We have already noted that Matthew, Mark and Luke present the Last Supper as a Passover *Seder*. In the following passage from Luke 22:14-20, Jesus is described as 'wanting to eat this Passover' meal, his last, with the apostles before his suffering and death. The passing around of the first cup at the beginning of the meal, the breaking and distribution of the bread and the passing around of 'the cup after supper' are also mentioned:

> And when the hour came, he reclined at table, and the apostles with him. And he said to them, 'I have earnestly desired to eat this Passover with you before I suffer; for I tell you I shall not eat it until it is fulfilled in the kingdom of God.' And he took a cup, and when he had given thanks he said, 'Take this, and divide it among yourselves; for I tell you that from now on I shall not drink of the fruit of the vine until the kingdom of God comes.' And he took bread, and when he had given thanks he broke it and gave it to them, saying, 'This is my body which is given for you. Do this in memory of me.' And likewise the cup after supper, saying, 'This cup which is poured out for you is the new covenant in my blood.'

Jesus identified the breaking and eating of the bread, and the pouring out and drinking of 'the cup after supper' with the gift of his Body and Blood in the Eucharist. The reference to 'before I suffer', the separate sections on eating bread/Body and drinking wine/Blood, and the description of the pouring out of the cup as 'the new covenant in my blood' clearly refer to his suffering and death. By making the Last Supper a Passover *Seder*, Luke invites us to interpret the death of Jesus on the cross with the slaughter of the Passover lamb and to interpret the saving power of painting the doorposts with the lamb's blood with the saving power of that death. The Passover *Seder* of unleavened bread, wine and roasted lamb commemorated the liberation of the people of Israel from slavery in Egypt and the eventual establishment of the covenant of Sinai. It made the events of the Exodus ritually present among them. By his command, 'Do this in memory of me', and by identifying his Body and Blood with the bread and wine, Jesus established the breaking and eating of bread, and the pouring and drinking of wine as the commemoration of his death and of the 'new covenant' in his blood.

Doing 'this' in memory of him makes the saving events of Holy Week ritually present among us. We too are invited to recognise the Eucharistic bread as his Body and the Eucharistic cup as his Blood. For Luke, the Last Supper was the fulfilment of what Passover had anticipated. The new covenant in the Blood of Jesus is the fulfilment of the Exodus from slavery and of the Sinai covenant. Luke describes Jesus as giving thanks (*'eucharistó'* in Greek), first for the wine and then for the bread. When we come to Mass, we too are invited to give thanks for the gift of the

Body and Blood of Jesus. We use the word 'Eucharist' to describe this sacrament because it expresses our gratitude for the events that it makes present again among us, the death and resurrection of Jesus that have liberated us from the slavery of sin and death.

The Pre-Passover Meal and the Mass

Matthew, Mark and Luke present the Last Supper as a Passover *Seder*. We have already noted, however, that it was probably a pre-Passover meal, as in the Gospel of John. The earliest surviving account of the Eucharist, 1 Corinthians 11:23-26, says that the Last Supper took place 'on the night when he was betrayed' and does not refer to Passover.

> For I received from the Lord what I also delivered to you, that the Lord Jesus on the night when he was betrayed took bread, and when he had given thanks, he broke it, and said, 'This is my body which is for you. Do this as a memorial of me.' In the same way also the cup, after supper, saying, 'This cup is the new covenant in my blood. Do this, as often as you drink it, as a memorial of me.' For as often as you eat this bread and drink the cup, you proclaim the Lord's death until he comes.

If it was, in fact, a pre-Passover meal, the bread may have been leavened and the 'supper' may not have consisted of roast lamb and bitter herbs. Eating bread and drinking wine was a normal feature of the evening meal. People ate with their hands and the head of the household normally said the thanksgiving and blessing at the beginning of the meal as he broke the bread and distributed it to those who were present. The version of the Jewish oral law, known as the Babylonian Talmud, notes that:

> Our Rabbis taught: A man should not break bread [i.e. recite the blessing] for visitors unless he eats with them, but he may break bread for his children and the members of his household so as to train them in the performance of religious duties.[6]

This text suggests that one of the purposes of the blessing said over the breaking of bread was to train people in the performance of their religious duties. Reared as an observant Jew, Paul may have interpreted what Jesus did at the Last Supper and his command, 'Do this in memory of me', as training the members of his new household in the performance of their religious duties.

The Fraternal Meal and the Eucharist[7]

When Jesus said, 'Do this in memory of me', was he referring only to the blessing for breaking the bread before the meal and to the blessing over the final cup at the end or was the meal itself also included? At the Last Supper, the meal came between the blessing over the bread and the blessing over the final cup of wine. Very soon, however, the meal came first (see 1 Cor 11:21, 33) and it was followed by the blessings over the breaking of bread and over the cup. By about the middle of the second

---

6 See Isidore Epstein, *The Soncino Babylonian Talmud* (London: Soncino Press, 1935–48), *Seder Mo'ed. Mas. Rosh Hashana*, 29b.

7 On the early history of the Eucharist, see Leo C. Hay OFM, *Eucharist: A Thanksgiving Celebration* (Message of the Sacraments, 3A) (Wilmington, Delaware: Michael Glazier Inc., 1989).

century, Eucharist was being celebrated in some places without a fraternal meal and this gradually became the norm. About AD 155, Justin Martyr made a clear distinction between the Eucharist and other kinds of food:

> We call this food Eucharist; and no one else is permitted to partake of it, except one who believes our teaching to be true and who has been washed in the washing which is for the remission of sins and for regeneration, and is thereby living as Christ has enjoined. For not as common bread or common drink do we receive those ...[8]

In the early centuries, there does not seem to have been a fixed formula for the blessings over the breaking of the bread and over the cup. By the early part of the third century, however, a set formula became more common, possibly in order to ensure that the essential elements were not omitted. The oldest certain version of the Eucharistic Prayer, the central prayer of the Mass, is found in the account of the Eucharist at the ordination of a Bishop in the *Apostolic Tradition* (3:4), written by Hippolytus c. AD 215. Although it is a long quotation, it is given here in full. Note the first three paragraphs leading up to the words of consecration and the final paragraph, which begins with the word 'remembering':[9]

> And when he has been made Bishop let every one offer him the kiss of peace, saluting him, for he has been made worthy. To him then let the Deacons

---

8 See Justin Martyr, *First Apology*, 66 in William A. Jurgens, *The Faith of the Early Fathers* (Collegeville, Minnesota: The Liturgical Press, 1970), 1:55.
9 See Jurgens, *The Faith of the Early Fathers*, 1:167 (394a).

bring the offerings and he with all the Presbyters laying his hand on the offerings shall say, giving thanks: 'The Lord be with you.' And the people shall say: 'And with your spirit.' 'Lift up your hearts.' 'We have them with the Lord.' 'Let us give thanks unto the Lord.' 'It is fitting and right.'

And then he shall continue immediately: 'We give you thanks, O God, through your beloved Son Jesus Christ whom, in the last time, you did send to us [to be] a Saviour and Redeemer and the Messenger of your will; who is your inseparable Word through whom you made all things and in whom you were well pleased; whom you did send from heaven into the Virgin's womb and who conceived within her was made flesh and was manifested as your Son, born of the Holy Spirit and a virgin; who fulfilling your will and winning for himself a holy people stretched forth his hands when it was time for him to suffer, so that, by his suffering, he might release from suffering those who have believed in you; who also, when he was betrayed to his voluntary suffering in order that he might abolish death and break the bonds of the devil and trample hell underfoot and enlighten the righteous and set a boundary[10] and show forth the resurrection: took bread and gave thanks to you, saying: "Take, eat: this is my body which is broken for you." Likewise also the cup, saying: "This is my blood which is poured out for you. Whenever you do this, you do it in memory of me."

---

10 *Terminum figat.*

21

Remembering, therefore, his death and resurrection, we offer to you the bread and the cup, giving thanks to you, because of your having accounted us worthy to stand before you and minister to you. And we pray that you might send your Holy Spirit upon the offering of the holy Church. Gather as one in the fullness of your Holy Spirit your saints who participate; and confirm their faith in truth so that we may praise and glorify you through your Son Jesus Christ, through whom be glory and honour to you, to the Father and the Son and the Holy Spirit, in your holy Church, both now and through the ages of ages. Amen.'

Over time, different forms of the Eucharistic Prayer developed and became the norm in particular places or regions. I will outline the four standard Eucharistic Prayers introduced after the Second Vatican Council in a later chapter. The Antiochene (Greek), Alexandrian (Coptic), Roman (Latin) and Gallican (also Latin, used in north-western Europe) rites for celebrating the Eucharist were recognisably distinct by the end of the fourth century. Many different rites for celebrating the Eucharist have survived and some are still in use.

The Development of the Mass[11]
In this section, I will outline the way in which the normal celebration of Mass in the Roman rite has developed

---

11 For further reading on the liturgical and historical aspects of the Mass, see Edward Schillebeeckx OP, *The Eucharist* (London: Sheet & Ward, 1968); J.D. Crichton, *Christian Celebration: Understanding the Mass* (Guildford: Biddles Ltd., revised edition 1993); Johannes H. Emminghaus, *The Eucharist: Essence, Form, Celebration* (Collegeville, Minnesota: Liturgical Press, revised edition 1997, part 1).

over the last fifteen hundred years or so. There are essentially three different periods: the Gregorian rite from about 600–1570; the Tridentine Rite from 1570–1970; and the Vatican II rite since then.

The Roman (Latin) liturgy[12] of the Mass was first codified by Pope St Gregory the Great (590–604). The Gregorian Rite simplified the existing Roman liturgy and established the definitive arrangement of the Eucharistic Prayer that is now known as the Roman Canon. The reading of texts from Scripture seems to have been part of the Eucharist from the beginning. Luke's account of the two disciples on the road to Emmaus describes Jesus as interpreting the Scriptures for them before they recognised him in the breaking of bread (see Lk 24:27). During the early centuries, the order of readings used seems to have followed that used in Jewish synagogues, but pride of place was now given to the Gospels and to the other texts of the New Testament. In the Gregorian Rite, the readings from Scripture to be used in the Mass were listed in a standardised Lectionary (collection of readings).[13] The Gregorian Rite had standardised forms for the introduction to the Mass, which included the Penitential Rites and the Opening Prayer, for the Communion Rites and for the Concluding Prayers and

---

12 As such, the Greek word 'liturgy' (leiturgia) means a public duty or service. It is used by Christians to describe the public or official service that the Church offers to God. In its broad sense, Roman Catholics use the word to describe all of its various rites and sacraments collectively, but it may also be used as a way of describing the Mass.

13 A **Lectionary** is a book containing all the readings used at Mass and at other liturgies, arranged according to the liturgical seasons (e.g. Ordinary Time, Lent, Eastertide, Advent, Christmas, etc.).

blessing. Following the blessing, the dismissal took the form: *'Ite, missa est'* (Go, it is ended) and the English word 'Mass' is thought to be derived from this dismissal.

Responding to both doctrinal and practical concerns that had been raised during the Protestant Reformation earlier that century, the Council of Trent (1545–63) appointed a commission to 'revise and restore' the Roman Missal.[14] In the new Missal of the Council of Trent, issued in 1570, uniformity was achieved by the suppression of regional variations and the doctrinal points that had been challenged by the Reformers were clearly affirmed. Daily Mass according to the Tridentine Missal included the use of incense at the beginning and during the offering of the gifts, and the 'Last Gospel' (Jn 1:1-14)[15] was read out in Latin at the end. The prayers of intercession for local needs, which had been part of the Gregorian Rite, were omitted. A new Roman Lectionary specifying what readings were to be used for different occasions was also issued in 1570. Generally speaking, there were two readings, the first only rarely from the Old Testament and the second from the Gospels. The readings were organised on a yearly cycle, with the same readings being used every year on a given Sunday or Feast Day. Most weekday Masses did not have their own

---

14 A **Missal** is a book containing the texts and prayers used during the celebration of Mass. Sometimes, the texts and prayers spoken by the celebrant, known as the **Sacramentary**, were distinguished from the Scripture readings that were used, known as the **Lectionary**, and, in some cases, the Sacramentary was published separately from the Lectionary.
15 This 'Last Gospel' seems to have been introduced into the Gregorian Rite during the Middle Ages.

proper readings, and the readings from the previous Sunday, or from the saint's day being celebrated, were used.

Recognising that the Tridentine Rite needed some adaptation to facilitate the active participation of the congregation attending Mass, the Second Vatican Council (1962–65) initiated a reform of the Roman liturgy. The result was the Missal of Pope Paul VI (1968). The importance of the readings from Scripture was highlighted by recognising that the Mass included a Liturgy of the Word as well as a Liturgy of the Eucharist. In addition to the Roman Canon, which was the only Eucharistic Prayer in the Tridentine Rite, three new Eucharistic Prayers were introduced. One of these was a reworking of the Eucharistic Prayer of Hippolytus (which we have noted at the end of the previous section). The prayers of intercession, as in the Gregorian Rite, were restored. A new Latin edition of the Roman Lectionary, based on a three-year cycle, was issued in 1969. The English version was published in 1970. A revised Latin edition of this Lectionary was issued in 1981 and the latest English version was published in the United States in 1998. Generally speaking, there are two proper readings for each daily Mass and three proper readings for Sunday Mass. The number of Old Testament readings has been increased significantly by comparison with the Tridentine Lectionary. The participation of the congregation is encouraged by the use of a series of responses, including a responsorial psalm after the first reading.

CHAPTER 2
THE CELEBRATION
OF MASS[1]

There are four basic parts to the Mass. Each is designed to help us to participate in the Eucharist as part of the local Christian community, to be nourished and strengthened in different ways by the Liturgy of the Word and by the Liturgy of the Eucharist, and to live our lives as a continual and communal worship of thanks and praise to God. The first part, the Preparatory Rites, and last part, the Concluding Rites, are essentially an introduction and a conclusion. The two major parts of the Mass are the Liturgy of the Word and the Liturgy of the Eucharist. To illustrate the structure of the Mass, and the way in which its different parts relate to each other, we take the example of the Evening Mass of the Lord's Supper on Holy Thursday. Since 1969, the celebration of Mass in the Roman Rite of the Catholic Church has been governed by the *General Instruction of the Roman Missal* (GIRM), which is often printed at the beginning of recent editions of the Roman Missal.[2]

---

1 See Johannes H. Emminghaus, *The Eucharist: Essence, Form, Celebration* (Collegeville, Minnesota: Liturgical Press, revised edition 1997); Enrico Mazza, *The Celebration of the Eucharist: The Origin of the Rite and the Development of its Interpretation* (Collegeville, Minnesota: Liturgical Press, 1999).
2 The version for England and Wales is available on the internet, see http://www.liturgyoffice.org.uk/Resources/GIRM/Documents/GIRM.pdf.

The Preparatory Rites

According to the *General Instruction of the Roman Missal*, the purpose of the Preparatory Rites is 'to ensure that the faithful, who come together as one, establish communion and dispose themselves to listen properly to God's word and to celebrate the Eucharist worthily' (GIRM 46). The different individuals and groups who prepare the church environment and those who have a particular ministry in the celebration of the Mass, such as choirs, have an important role to play here. As well as ensuring that there is sufficient heat and light, and that the altar cloths and utensils are clean and serviceable, the message and themes of each particular Mass should be reflected in the way the church is decorated and in the choice of music. The Mass of the Lord's Supper, which begins the solemn three-day celebration of the death and resurrection of Jesus, commemorates the institution of the Eucharist and of the Sacrament of Orders, as well as the new commandment of brotherly love that Jesus gave after washing the feet of his disciples. As this Mass begins, the tabernacle should be empty and open, and it remains so during Good Friday and Holy Saturday. Before Mass begins, silence should be observed in the church and in the sacristy and adjacent areas, 'so that all may dispose themselves to carry out the sacred action in a devout and fitting manner' (GIRM 45).

As well as opening the celebration and accompanying the procession of the Priest and ministers, the **Entrance Hymn** is intended to unite the many different individuals who are present into a single congregation, singing or listening to words that 'introduce their thoughts to the mystery of the liturgical season or festivity' (GIRM 47).

The hymn should be chosen to suit the Mass of the Lord's Supper and, if all are expected to join in, it should either be easy to sing or have a 'chorus'.

If there is no entrance hymn, the **Entrance Antiphon** for the Mass is read or incorporated into the celebrant's introduction (GIRM 31, 48). The antiphon is a quotation from Scripture or another text that focuses our attention on the principal theme of that Mass. The Entrance Antiphon for Holy Thursday, based on Galatians 6:14, reminds us that we are beginning the three-day celebration of the death and resurrection of Jesus: 'We should glory in the cross of our Lord Jesus Christ, for he is our salvation, our life and our resurrection; through him we are saved and made free.'

Jesus revealed to us that God is a trinity of divine Persons and we know that all Christians are baptised in the name of the Father, the Son and the Holy Spirit (see Mt 28:19). The **Sign of the Cross** at the beginning of Mass reminds us that every celebration of the Mass is a prayer invoking the name of the Blessed Trinity.

The **Greeting** and response recognise that Jesus, the risen and glorified Lord, is always present when two or three are gathered in his name (see Mt 18:20).

The **Penitential Rite** prepares us to hear the Word of God and to receive the Eucharist by reminding us that only God's mercy and grace make us worthy to participate. Following 'a brief pause for silence' (GIRM 51), it provides an opportunity in a public setting for the general confession of minor transgressions that do not need to be confessed in the sacrament of Penance. The

'Kyrie eleison' (Greek for 'Lord, have mercy'), i.e. the 'Lord, have mercy ... Christ, have mercy ... Lord, have mercy', asks the risen Lord to have mercy on our sins. Based on an ancient litany, it is Jesus who is addressed in each case (rather than Father, Son and Spirit).

The **Gloria** is an ancient hymn of joy that is sung or said on Sundays outside the seasons of Advent and Lent and on important feasts. It highlights the humanity of Christ, his redemptive death and resurrection ('you take away the sin of the world') and his role as our mediator with God the Father ('you are seated at the right hand of the Father, receive our prayer'). The church bells are rung during the singing of the 'Gloria' on Holy Thursday and they then remain silent until the Easter Vigil.

The **Opening Prayer** expresses the general or overall theme of that particular celebration of the Mass. Having invited the people to pray, there is a 'brief silence' before the Priest gathers together (the original name for this prayer was the 'Collect') all the desires and petitions of the individuals present in this prayer. Many of the Opening Prayers used in the Mass come from ancient Mass texts, but the Opening Prayer for Holy Thursday was newly composed for the 1962 Missal. It presents the Last Supper as a new revelation of God's love for us and a new Passover in which Christ, 'our Paschal lamb', is sacrificed (see 1 Cor 5:7-8). It prays that, by celebrating it, we may come to the fullness of life (see Jn 10:10): 'God our Father, we are gathered here to share in the supper which your only Son left to his Church to reveal his love. He gave it to us when he was about to die and commanded us to celebrate it as the new and eternal sacrifice. We pray that in this Eucharist we may find the fullness of love and life.'

The Liturgy of the Word

According to the General Instruction on the Roman Missal, the readings from the Bible are the main part of the Liturgy of the Word and non-biblical texts may never be substituted for the lectionary texts (GIRM 55, 57) because, in the biblical texts, God speaks to his people about their redemption and salvation. Christ is present in his Word and he provides us with spiritual nourishment through that Word as well as through the sacrament of the Eucharist itself. We make God's word our own by listening to it attentively, by joining in the responses and by responding to the words that God has addressed to us.

The services held in Jewish synagogues on the Sabbath had two Old Testament readings, the first from Genesis, Exodus, Numbers, Deuteronomy or Leviticus, and the second from the Prophets, followed by a homily that explained the readings. Jesus was probably familiar with this structure since he usually attended the Sabbath service in the local synagogue (see Lk 4:16). Although the New Testament is now included and the Gospels are given pride of place, our Liturgy of the Word has its roots in those synagogue services. Because the arrangement of the biblical readings is designed to highlight the unity of the Old and New Testaments, the arrangement of the biblical readings in the Liturgy of the Word should normally be maintained (GIRM 57).

If there is a Second Reading, the **First Reading** is usually from the Old Testament (or from the Acts of the Apostles during Eastertide). Except for the first part of Advent, when the Gospel is chosen to suit the prophetic text of the First Reading, the First Reading is chosen to suit the Gospel of the day. The function of proclaiming the first and second readings is not reserved to the one who presides at the Eucharist (GIRM 59) and these readings are normally read by an instituted Lector or by extraordinary ministers of the Word. The First Reading for Holy Thursday (Exodus 12:1-8, 11-14) presents the ceremony of the Passover Lamb as a commemoration of the liberation of the people of Israel from their slavery in Egypt. Putting the lamb's blood on their doorposts reminded the people of Israel that God had spared them from the plague that destroyed the firstborn of the Egyptians. It reminds us that, in order to set us free from sin and death, God the Father did not spare his only begotten Son. In his Last Supper, Jesus became our Passover Lamb and it is through his blood that we have been saved. Recognising this reading from Exodus commanding us to celebrate the sacrifice of the Passover Lamb as God's own words addressed to us here and now, the reader says: 'This is the word of the Lord'. Welcoming the fact that God has spoken to us in and through this reading, we reply: 'Thanks be to God'.

The **Responsorial Psalm** is an opportunity to meditate on the First Reading by reflecting on the parallels between the celebration of Passover and our Eucharist. Ancient Jewish rabbis associated Psalms 113–118 with the final cup of wine drunk during the Passover meal and, in that context, taking the 'cup of salvation' (Ps 115:4) and the promise to offer 'a sacrifice of thanksgiving' in the Temple (Ps 115:8) were probably understood as aspects of the communal celebration of the Jewish Passover. In the Responsorial Psalm for Holy Thursday, 'cup of salvation' and 'sacrifice of thanksgiving' refer to the communal celebration of our Christian Eucharist. The response to the Psalm, which is normally sung by the entire congregation, is an opportunity to express how the Psalm reflects on the First Reading. The response for Holy Thursday identifies the 'cup of salvation', mentioned in the psalm (Ps 115:4), with the cup that is blessed in the Eucharist, mentioned by St Paul (1 Cor 10:16): 'The blessing cup that we bless is a communion with the blood of Christ.' We offer our sacrifice of 'thanksgiving' ('eucharistia' in Greek) by breaking the bread and blessing the cup as Jesus commanded. It is the means by which we enter into communion with him.

The **Second Reading** is usually taken from the New Testament. Sometimes it focuses on a theme that is already found in the First Reading or in the Gospel. At other times, it focuses on a sub-theme that has no direct connection with either of the other readings. On Holy Thursday, the second reading is the earliest recorded account of the institution of the Eucharist (1 Cor 11:23-26). Jesus commanded us to break bread and to bless the cup in his memory and, in this way, to proclaim his saving death until he returns in glory: 'Every time you eat this bread and drink this cup, you are proclaiming the Lord's death until he comes.' The Mass is not just a way of remembering Jesus. It is the means by which his saving life, death and resurrection become powerfully present in our lives as we await his return in glory.

The **Gospel Acclamation** welcomes the Good News that the Gospel proclaims in Christ's name. We sit for the other readings but we stand for the Gospel Acclamation and for the Gospel itself to mark the special presence of the risen Jesus whenever the Gospel is proclaimed. The acclamation usually begins and ends with the singing of the word 'Alleluia', a Hebrew word meaning 'Praise the Lord (God)' that is found at the beginning of many of the psalms of praise.[3] In keeping with the more sombre mood of Lent, this joyful word is not used and it is replaced by an equivalent phrase, such as 'Praise and honour to you, Lord Jesus Christ'. The verse between the 'Alleluias' sums up the central message of the Gospel reading. On Holy Thursday, it is 'I give you a new commandment: love one another just as I have loved you, says the Lord' (Jn 13:34). The 'commandment' mentioned here, *'mandatum'* in Latin or *'mandé'* in French, is the origin of the old name for Holy Thursday, 'Maundy' Thursday. Jesus loved us and became our Passover Lamb to liberate us from the power of sin and death. He is the measure of authentic loving and, united in communion with his love through the Eucharist, we are commanded to love one another just as he has loved us.

The **Gospel** is the central focus and the key text of the Liturgy of the Word. To highlight its importance, the dialogue before the Gospel reminds us that the risen Lord is present among us when we listen to the Gospel being proclaimed. In response to the announcement that

---

3 The liturgical hymn known as the 'Sequence', which is optional except on Easter Sunday and on Pentecost Day, is sung before the 'Alleluia'.

the Gospel is about to be read, we anticipate its proclamation of the Good News of our Lord, Jesus Christ, in the response: 'Glory to you, Lord.' Traditionally, people make the sign of the cross on their foreheads, lips and chest during this response. This practice seems to have developed in imitation of the Priest or Deacon who blessed himself in this way before reading the Gospel, praying that God would be in his mind, on his lips and in his heart when he was reading it. The Gospel for Holy Thursday (Jn 13:1-15) highlights the deeper meaning of the death and resurrection of Jesus, and of the institution of the Eucharist. Taking on the work that was normally done by a slave, Jesus washed the feet of his disciples, aware that one of them was about to betray him. When Peter objected, Jesus told him that he could have 'no part' in what Jesus had come to do unless he allowed Jesus to wash his feet. He told them that they should follow the example of their Lord and Master by washing one another's feet. Like Peter, we can have 'no part' in what Jesus came to do unless we allow him to wash our feet and unless we are willing to wash the feet of others. At the conclusion of the reading, the Priest or Deacon says: 'This is the Gospel of the Lord.' By our response, 'Praise to you, Lord Jesus Christ', we express our praise and thanksgiving for the Good News of the Gospel that we have just heard.

The **Homily** 'should be an exposition of some aspect of the readings from Sacred Scripture or of another text from the Ordinary or from the Proper of the Mass of the day and should take into account both the mystery being celebrated and the particular needs of the listeners' (GIRM 65). Normally given by the Priest celebrant himself, it may be entrusted to another Priest or to the Deacon, but 'never to a lay person' (GIRM 66). The homily for the Mass of the Lord's Supper might focus on the new commandment of brotherly love that Jesus gave after washing the feet of his disciples, on the institution of the Eucharist or on the institution of the sacrament of Orders.

The Collection is often taken up after the homily. In Romans 15:27, Paul describes the material help, which the Gentile Churches were giving to the Church in Jerusalem, as 'ministering [*leitourgesai*] to them in material things'. The collection is an important part of the liturgy, inviting us and giving us the opportunity to offer material support to those in need as well as to the various ministries of the Church.

In the **Profession of Faith, or Creed,** the whole gathered people give assent to the Word of God that they have heard in the readings and in the homily by calling to mind and professing the central mysteries of the faith. The Creed was originally used as a summary of the faith during adult Baptism and it was first used in Mass during the sixth century in the East. It spread to Spain and Ireland and, thanks to the missionary work of Irish monks in the kingdom of the Franks, it reached Rome in the eleventh century. For the next nine hundred years, the Roman Rite included the recitation of the Creed on all solemn feasts of the Lord, including Holy Thursday. In 1955, the liturgical reforms under Pope Pius XII returned to the earlier Roman tradition on this point and, since then, the Profession of Faith is not said on Holy Thursday.

The **General Intercessions**, which are also known as the
Prayers of the Faithful, are a response to the Word of God
in which the people of God exercise their priestly function
by interceding for all humanity (GIRM 69). Following a
short introduction in which the celebrant invites all
present to pray, the intentions normally include prayers
for the needs of the Church, for public authorities, for the
salvation of the world and of all humanity, for those
oppressed by any need and for the local community
(GIRM 70). The intentions should be expressed in a
restrained, distinct and brief style, and they should take
the needs of the whole community into account (GIRM
71).

The Liturgy of the Eucharist[4]
The Liturgy of the Word is focused on the ambo or lectern
where the Word was read. The part of the Mass known as
the Liturgy of the Eucharist (in the strict sense of the
term) is focused on the altar, which is both the place
where the sacrifice of Jesus is made present among us
and the table for the sacred meal of the Body and Blood.
According to Vatican II's *Constitution on the Sacred
Liturgy* (56), 'the liturgy of the Word and the liturgy of the
Eucharist are so closely bound up with each other that
they amount to one single act of worship'. The God
whom we worship by listening to the Liturgy of the Word
became Incarnate in Jesus, our Lord, and we worship
him by celebrating the Liturgy of the Eucharist as he
commanded us.

---

4 See Raymond Moloney SJ, *The Eucharistic Prayers in Worship, Preaching
and Study* (Dublin: Dominican Publications, 1985).

The Liturgy of the Eucharist begins with the **Presentation of the Gifts**. As well as offerings for the poor, for example, the principal gifts are the bread and wine that will become the Lord's Body and Blood. The prayer of offering reminds us that Jesus united himself with our humanity and gave us his Body and Blood so that we might enter into communion with his divinity: 'By the mystery of this water and wine may we come to share in the divinity of Christ who humbled himself to share in our humanity.' The prayer thanks God for the fruits of the earth and of the vine that we offer: 'Blessed are you, Lord, God of all creation. Through your goodness we have this bread/wine to offer ...' The prayer describes the bread and wine as 'the work of human hands' and the human effort involved is part of the sacrifice we offer. It is appropriate, therefore, that we offer our own daily life and work to God together with the bread and wine and that we ask God to accept and bless our sacrifice: 'Pray, brethren that our sacrifice may be acceptable ... May the Lord accept the sacrifice at your hands ...'

The **Prayer over the gifts** is usually related to the theme of the Mass and it relates this theme to the situation of those present. For Holy Thursday, the prayer is based on Vatican II's Decree on the Liturgy, *Sacrosanctum concilium* (2), which says that the work of our redemption is accomplished especially in the divine sacrifice of the Eucharist: 'Lord, make us worthy to celebrate these mysteries. Each time we offer this memorial sacrifice the work of our redemption is accomplished.'

The **Eucharistic Prayer** is a prayer of 'thanksgiving and sanctification' that is the 'centre and summit' of the celebration of Mass (GIRM 78). In Greek, it is known as the *'anaphora'* (offering), the formal offering of the sacrifice, and in the Latin tradition it was known as the *'canon actionis'* (the order of the proceedings). It begins with a dialogue between the celebrant and the faithful, based on the Eucharistic Prayer in the *Apostolic Tradition* (c. AD 215) by Hippolytus, which was quoted towards the end of chapter 1, inviting us to 'lift up' our hearts because of the great things that God has done for his people. The Preface can vary depending on the liturgical season and the preface for Holy Thursday reminds us that Jesus is 'the true and eternal Priest, who founded this memorial of his unending sacrifice'. Made present among us at every Mass, his sacrifice continues to purify and strengthen us: 'As we eat his body, given for us, we grow in strength. As we drink his blood, poured out for us, we are washed clean, and are joined together in his covenant of love.' The preface ends with the 'Holy, Holy, Holy', a chant echoing the worship of Jesus by the angels in heaven (see Isa 6:1-8) and the way Jesus was welcomed into Jerusalem with palms and the singing of 'Hosanna'.

Several different Eucharistic Prayers are now used during Mass, but the most common are Eucharistic Prayers I, II, III and IV. The first is based on the traditional Roman Eucharistic Prayer or 'canon'. Eucharistic Prayer II, which is also the shortest, is based on the version found in the *Apostolic Tradition* by Hippolytus. The third Eucharistic Prayer was newly composed after Vatican II (1962–65), based on older prayers. Since it can be combined with a wide variety of different prefaces, it is often used on Sundays and Holy Days. Based on very ancient texts, many of which reflect Eastern (especially Greek) traditions, Eucharistic Prayer IV is longer than the others and it has a richer account of salvation history. It has its own (unchangeable) preface.

The **Invocation or *Epiclesis*** calls on the Holy Spirit to transform the gifts of bread and wine so that they may become the Body and Blood of our Lord, Jesus Christ. In Eucharistic Prayer II, for example, the invocation includes the words, 'Let your Spirit come upon these gifts to make them holy, so that they may become for us the body and blood of our Lord, Jesus Christ.' In the First Eucharist Prayer, the invocation is implicit in the celebrant's body posture, with the hands facing upwards, when he prays that the offered gifts 'become the body and blood of Jesus Christ'.

During the **Consecration**, the celebrant repeats the words of Jesus when he instituted the Eucharist: 'This is my body ... this is my blood.' Because of his Priestly ordination, the celebrant acts 'in the person of Christ' (*in persona Christi*) when he invokes the Holy Spirit over the gifts and when he says the words of institution.[5] The invocation of the Spirit and the words of institution have the same transforming effect that they did at the Last Supper. The bread, which still looks and tastes like bread, becomes his Body and the wine, which still looks and tastes like wine, becomes his Blood. No bread or wine remains. Their 'substance' has been irreversibly changed.

---

5 The Western Church's emphasis on the words of Consecration and the Eastern Church's emphasis on the invocation of the Holy Spirit do not constitute mutually exclusive positions and, since Vatican II, the Western Liturgy has been careful to include an explicit invocation of the Spirit in its new Eucharistic Prayers.

To recognise that the Body and Blood of the risen Jesus were present on the altar after the Consecration, an acclamation known as the **Memorial Acclamation** was introduced at this point in the Mass in 1969. There are four different forms of this Acclamation, each proclaiming the saving power of Christ's death and resurrection as we await his return in glory:

- Christ has died, Christ is risen, Christ will come again.
- Dying you destroyed our death, rising you restored our life. Lord Jesus, come in glory.
- When we eat this bread and drink this cup, we proclaim your death, Lord Jesus, until you come in glory.
- Lord, by your cross and resurrection, you have set us free. You are the Saviour of the World.

Jesus told us to celebrate the Eucharist in his memory and **the prayer remembering the death, resurrection and ascension of Jesus** is addressed to God the Father. In the First Eucharistic Prayer, this prayer includes the words: 'Father, we celebrate the memory of Christ, your Son. We ... recall his passion, his resurrection from the dead, and his ascension into glory.' In Eucharistic Prayer IV it takes the following form: 'Father, we now celebrate this memorial of our redemption. We recall Christ's death, his descent among the dead, his resurrection, and his ascension to your right hand.'

The **prayer for unity** takes the following form in the fourth Eucharistic Prayer: 'Lord, look upon this sacrifice which you have given to your Church; and by your Holy Spirit, gather all who share this bread and wine into the one body of Christ, a living sacrifice of praise.' In the second Eucharistic Prayer, the Spirit is invoked so that 'we, who are nourished by his body and blood, may be filled with his Holy Spirit, and may become one body, one spirit in Christ'. Before the Consecration, the celebrant invoked the Holy Spirit over the bread and wine to enable them to become the Body and Blood of Jesus. After the Consecration, the celebrant invokes the Holy Spirit over the congregation, asking that we may become one Body in Christ through sharing the one Eucharist. The Eucharist makes the risen Jesus present on the altar but that is not its ultimate purpose. By eating his Body and by drinking his Blood we are filled with his Spirit and we enter into a deeper and more profound unity with Jesus and with one another.

There are **intercessions for the dead and for sinners** in the first three Eucharistic Prayers. In the second Eucharistic Prayer they take the following form: 'Remember our brothers and sisters who have gone to their rest in the hope of rising again; bring them and all the departed into the light of your presence. Have mercy on us all; make us worthy to share eternal life with Mary, the virgin Mother of God, with the apostles, and with all the saints who have done your will throughout the ages. May we praise you in union with them, and give you glory through your Son, Jesus Christ.'

The Eucharistic Prayer ends with a hymn of praise, giving glory to the Father through the Son in the Holy Spirit. The congregation express their approval of this offering of praise, and of all that has been done throughout the Eucharistic Prayer, by the word 'Amen', meaning 'so be it'.

After the Eucharistic Prayer, the Liturgy of the Eucharist continues with the **Communion Rite**, in which we are brought into communion with Jesus through eating his Body and drinking his Blood.

The Communion Rite begins with the **Lord's Prayer**, the model for all prayer given to us by Jesus himself. As part of the Communion Rite, the petition asking God the Father for 'our daily bread' reminds us that we need the spiritual nourishment of the Eucharistic Bread. The petition asking for forgiveness reminds us that we need God's forgiveness and that we must be willing to forgive one another, if we are to truly become one body in Christ through the Eucharist. The **Embolism** or insertion, 'Deliver us, Lord, from all evil ...', develops the last petition of the Lord's Prayer, asking that the entire community of the faithful may be delivered from the power of evil. The congregation concludes the Embolism by saying the ancient prayer of praise that Anglicans and other Protestants usually add to the Lord's Prayer, 'For the kingdom, the power and the glory are yours now and forever'.

In the **Rite of Peace**, which begins, 'Lord, Jesus Christ, your said to your apostles, I leave you peace ...', the Church 'asks for peace and unity for herself and for the whole human family, and the faithful express to each other their ecclesial communion and mutual charity before communicating in the Sacrament'. The manner in which the sign of peace is given can vary in accordance with local culture and customs, but it should be offered 'in a sober manner' only to those nearest to us (GIRM 82).

The **Breaking of the Eucharistic Bread**, a term used to describe the whole celebration of the Eucharist in apostolic times (see Acts 2:42), 'signifies that the many faithful are made one body (1 Cor 10:17) by receiving Communion from the one Bread of Life which is Christ, who died and rose for the salvation of the world' (GIRM 83). The Priest puts a piece of the host into the chalice to signify the unity of the living and glorious Body and Blood of the Lord in the work of salvation. This rite is accompanied by a chant, based on John 1:29, asking that Jesus, our Paschal Lamb, may liberate us from the power of sin: 'Lamb of God, you take away the sins of the world, have mercy on us/grant us peace.'

Following a prayer that he may receive the Body and Blood of Christ fruitfully, the Priest presents the Eucharistic Bread to the faithful, holding it above the paten or above the chalice. As he does so, he invites them to recognise that they are, in fact, present at the new Passover of the Lord's Supper: '**Behold the Lamb of God** who takes away the sins of the world, happy are those who are called to his supper.' Together, using the words of the centurion (Mt 8:8), Priest and people acknowledge that it is only the loving mercy of Jesus that makes them worthy to be present: '**Lord, I am not worthy** to receive you but only say the word and I shall be healed.'

If a sung **Communion chant** is to accompany the procession to receive Communion, it begins as the Priest is receiving the sacrament and continues for as long as Communion is being given to the faithful. If there is no singing, the **Communion Antiphon** is said following the

Priest's Communion. On Holy Thursday, the antiphon recalls the institution of the Eucharist at the Last Supper: 'This body will be given for you. This is the cup of the new covenant in my blood; whenever you receive them, do so in remembrance of me.'

Responding 'Amen' to the invitation, 'The body of Christ', the faithful may choose to receive the host on the tongue or in the hand. Because receiving communion in the hand was a relative novelty when it was reintroduced after the Second Vatican Council, some people think that, up until then, people always received communion on the tongue. This is not the case as can be seen from the way in which the fourth-century St Cyril of Jerusalem describes the attitudes and manner of receiving communion:

> When you come up to receive the Lord, make your left hand a throne for your right, since your right hand is about to welcome a king. Cup your palm and receive in it Christ's body, saying in response, 'Amen' ... Then, after receiving the body of Christ, go over to the chalice of his blood. Do not reach out [immediately], but bow in a gesture of adoration and veneration and answer 'Amen'.[6]

When both the host and the chalice are distributed to the faithful, people may choose whether to receive from the chalice or not. At the invitation of the minister, 'The blood of Christ', the communicant responds, 'Amen'.

---

6 St Cyril of Jerusalem, *Mystagogical Catecheses*, 5:21–22.

When the distribution of Communion is finished, as circumstances suggest, the Priest and faithful spend some time praying quietly. If desired, a psalm or other canticle of praise or a hymn may also be sung by the entire congregation. (GIRM 88)

The Communion Rite ends with the **Prayer after Communion**, which prays that the Eucharist just celebrated may bear fruit. If the Sunday is part of a particular liturgical season (Lent/Advent), this prayer relates this particular Eucharist with that liturgical season. On Holy Thursday, the Prayer after Communion is: 'Almighty God, we receive new life from the supper your Son gave us in this world. May we find full contentment in the meal we hope to share in your kingdom.'

The Concluding Rites
The Concluding Rites begin with brief announcements, if these are necessary. Such announcements might include any arrangements about the times of Masses for the coming week. These announcements are followed by a prayer asking that the Lord remain with us, 'The Lord be with you. And also with you', and the **Blessing** in the name of the Father, the Son and the Holy Spirit, to which the faithful reply, 'Amen'. On certain days, and on other occasions, a longer and more solemn Blessing is used in which the faithful reply 'Amen' to each of the prayers.

The **Dismissal** of the people by the Deacon or Priest sends them out 'to do good works, praising and blessing God' (GIRM 90): 'The Mass is ended. Go in peace [to love and serve the Lord].' Giving thanks to God that our communion with the risen Christ has enabled us to love and serve him, the faithful respond, 'Thanks be to God'.

The Priest and Deacon kiss the altar, and the Priest, Deacon and other ministers make a profound bow to the altar before they process out. Although not, as such, part of the official rites of the Mass, the procession of the ministers is often accompanied by a **Final Hymn** that recalls the message of the readings or the sense of being commissioned in the Dismissal.

When another liturgy follows Mass, the Concluding Rites are omitted. On Holy Thursday, for example, the transfer of the Holy Eucharist to the 'Altar of Repose', accompanied by a suitable procession and hymns, replaces the Concluding Rites.

CHAPTER 3
DIFFERENT ROLES AND FUNCTIONS DURING MASS

This third chapter describes the different roles and functions of both clergy and lay people when the Eucharist is celebrated. In addition to the celebrant and concelebrants, the Deacons, Acolytes, Lectors, the Extraordinary Ministers of the Word and of Holy Communion all have a particular role. There are also musicians, singers and others who help in different ways. The assembled congregation should also participate actively, rather than passively, in the sacramental action.

At weekend Masses, there are often concelebrating Priests; the first and second readings are done by Extraordinary Ministers of the Word; Extraordinary Ministers of Holy Communion help to distribute Communion; and there are usually some musicians and singers. Many people are, perhaps, less familiar with the roles of Deacons, Acolytes and Lectors. By means of their various roles and functions, all these different individuals help the assembled congregation to become more than merely passive observers, to hear God's Word and to make it their own, to unite their lives with the self-offering of Jesus on the altar and to enter into a deeper communion with the risen Lord in Holy Communion.

The Congregation

The celebration of the Eucharist is an action of the whole Church, the People of God that have been purchased by Christ's Blood, gathered together by the Lord and nourished by his Word. In the celebration of Mass, the faithful form a holy people, a people whom God has made his own, a royal priesthood, so that they may give thanks to God and offer the spotless Victim not only through the hands of the Priest, but also together with him, and so that they may learn to offer themselves. They continually grow in holiness by their conscious, active and fruitful participation in the mystery of the Eucharist.[1]

During the Mass, the people participate directly or indirectly in all that takes place. The entrance hymn both expresses and fosters the unity of the congregation that has gathered for Mass and the Priest makes the Sign of the Cross together with the whole gathering. The people's response, 'And also with you', to the celebrant's greeting, 'The Lord be with you', recognises Christ's presence among his people and it manifests the mystery of the Church gathered together for this particular celebration of Mass. Ordinarily, the *'Kyrie eleison'* is said or sung by the entire congregation. The 'Gloria' may be sung by the choir but it is normally said or sung by everyone together. The Opening Prayer, the Prayer over the Offerings and the Prayer after Communion, which are known as the Presidential Prayers, are addressed to God by the Priest who presides in the name of the entire People of God and in the name of all present. The people

---

1 See GIRM 5, 95.

make these prayers their own when they respond 'Amen'. God's Word is addressed to the people during the readings and the people make it their own by their silence and by their response to the Psalm. They acknowledge that Christ is present in the ordained minister and in the congregation before the Gospel is proclaimed.

Nourished by the Word of God, it is their petitions for the needs of the Church and for the salvation of the world that are expressed in the Prayer of the Faithful. The Creed is said or sung by the Priest together with the people. When the gifts that have been brought to the altar are incensed as a sign of the Church's offerings and prayer rising like incense in the sight of God, the people may be incensed to highlight their common baptismal dignity. At the beginning of the Eucharistic Prayer, the Priest invites the people to lift up their hearts to the Lord in prayer and thanksgiving, uniting the congregation with himself in the Prayer that he addresses in the name of the entire community to God the Father through Jesus Christ in the Holy Spirit. Joining with the angels in heaven, the whole congregation says or sings the 'Holy, Holy, Holy'. After the consecration, the people say or sing the Memorial Acclamation. By their 'Amen' at the end of the Eucharistic Prayer, the people affirm and approve all that takes place during that prayer. The Lord's Prayer is said by the Priest together with the entire congregation. After the Embolism, said by the Priest, the people conclude with a prayer glorifying God: 'For the kingdom, the power and the glory are yours, now and forever.' Having exchanged the greeting of peace with the Priest, the people offer the sign of peace to those who are nearest to them in accordance with locally approved custom. The congregation either recite the 'Lamb of God' or sing it with the choir and cantor, and they say the 'Lord, I am not worthy' with the Priest. They sometimes sing a psalm or some other canticle of praise when the distribution of Communion is finished. At the conclusion of Mass, the congregation is blessed by the Priest and sent out to do good works, praising and blessing God.[2]

On occasion, a member of the faithful may be asked to perform a particular ministry or role during the celebration of Mass and the *General Instruction on the Roman Missal* recommends that the faithful not refuse to serve the People of God in this way whenever they are asked to do so.[3]

The Celebrant and Concelebrants
Only those who have been ordained as Priests (presbyters) possess within the Church the power of Holy Orders to offer sacrifice in the person of Christ. It is for this reason that the Priest stands at the head of the faithful people who have gathered to celebrate Mass, that he presides over their prayer, proclaims the message of salvation to them, associates the people with himself in offering the sacrifice and gives them the Bread of Eternal Life. Since the Priest acts in the person of Christ, who offered this sacrifice to unite the Church to himself as his Body, the celebration of the Eucharist is always an action of Christ and the Church, the holy people who are united

---

2 See GIRM 30, 47, 50, 52–5, 68, 75, 78–9, 81–3, 88, 90, 129, 134, 137, 151–5, 157, 167, 216.
3 See GIRM 97.

in hierarchical communion under their Bishops. Every legitimate celebration of the Mass, in fact, is directed by the local Bishop, either in person or through the Priests who are his helpers.[4]

In the last chapter, we outlined the different functions of the Priest celebrant during Mass. If there are concelebrants, one and the same Priest, the principal celebrant, presides at the Mass and carries out all the duties assigned to the presiding celebrant, including the Presidential Prayers (the Opening Prayer, the Prayer over the Offerings and the Prayer after Communion). The non-presidential functions of the celebrant may be done by the concelebrating Priests. The presiding celebrant wears a chasuble. The concelebrating Priests, who walk ahead of the president celebrant in the procession, wear a chasuble or a stole. The principal celebrant says the prayers assigned to the celebrant during the preparatory rites. One of the concelebrants may read the Gospel and give the homily. The preparation of the gifts is done by the principal celebrant who also says the prayer over the offerings. The preface is said or sung by the principal celebrant alone and only he makes the usual gestures during the Eucharistic Prayer. To ensure that the words are clearly understood by the people, the parts spoken by all the concelebrants together, and especially the words of consecration, which all are bound to say, are to be said in such a way that the concelebrants speak them in a very low voice and that the principal celebrant's voice is clearly heard. The prayers of the celebrant during the

---

4 See GIRM 91–3.

Communion Rite are said by the principal celebrant alone, but one of the concelebrants may invite the people to exchange the sign of peace when no Deacon is present. The concelebrants may also assist in the breaking of the Eucharistic bread. The concelebrants receive communion under both species immediately after the principal celebrant does so. They may receive from the chalice by intinction (dipping the host in the chalice).[5]

The Deacon
The office of Deacon (servant) seems to have begun with the seven men, including Stephen, who are described as taking charge of the charitable work of the early Church in chapter 6 of the Acts of the Apostles. The qualities expected of Deacons, and of their households, are described in 1 Timothy 3:8-13. Although it figures prominently in the early centuries of the Church, the Deaconate as a permanent ministry gradually disappeared and, in the period leading up to Vatican II, the only Deacons were those in the final stages of preparation for ordination as Priests (presbyters). Vatican II recommended the restoration of permanent Deacons (see *Lumen gentium* 29) and, since then, permanent Deacons, many of them married, have become commonplace in many countries. In the last few years, permanent Deacons were also introduced in Ireland.

During Mass, Deacons, who either wear a dalmatic or a stole worn over the left shoulder (rather than around the

---

5 See GIRM 108, 199–251.

neck), assist the Priest in different ways as well as having other particular responsibilities. During the entrance procession, they either walk beside the Priest or precede him carrying the *Book of the Gospels*. Like the Priest, a Deacon venerates the altar with a kiss. If incense is used, Deacons assist the Priest by putting some into the thurible and they then take their place beside the Priest. If no suitable reader is present, Deacons may read the readings that precede the Gospel. During the 'Alleluia', they make a profound bow before the Priest, asking in a low voice, 'Father, give me your blessing', and they make the sign of the cross and say, 'Amen' after they are blessed by the Priest, who says, 'The Lord be in your heart'. Taking the *Book of the Gospels* from the altar, he places it on the ambo and incenses it just before he proclaims the Gospel. After the Prayer of the Faithful, whose intentions are normally announced by the Deacon, he prepares the altar, placing the sacred vessels on the altar, and he assists the Priests in receiving the gifts. Adding a little water to the chalice, the Deacon presents the bread and the chalice to the Priest. At the conclusion of the Eucharistic Prayer, the Deacon holds up the chalice and the Priest holds the paten during the final doxology, 'Through him, with him and in him ...' The Deacon may invite the faithful to exchange the sign of peace. Deacons receive Communion under both species after the Priest(s) and they assist the Priest in distributing Communion to the people, administering the chalice to the communicants if Communion is given under both kinds. When all have received from the chalice, he immediately and reverently consumes all that remains in the chalice at the altar, assisted if necessary by other Deacons and Priests. The Deacon purifies the vessels either when the distribution of Communion is completed or immediately after Mass. If there are brief announcements after the Prayer of Communion, the Deacon may do them if the Priest does not do them himself. If there is going to be a solemn blessing, the Deacon says, 'Bow your heads and pray for God's blessing'. After the Priest's blessing, the Deacon dismisses the people with the words, 'The Mass is ended, go in peace'.[6]

Acolytes and Lectors

In 1965, Vatican II's Decree on the Apostolate of Lay People, *Apostolicam actuositatem* (10), recognised that 'the laity have an active part of their own in the life and action of the Church' and that 'without it [their action] the apostolate of the pastors will frequently be unable to obtain its full effect'. In order to enable the laity to exercise a liturgical ministry, an Apostolic Letter of Pope Paul VI in 1972[7] allowed lay men to be instituted permanently as Acolytes (attendants) or Lectors (readers). When they exercise these roles during the celebration of Mass, they wear an alb[8] and take their place in the sanctuary with the ordained ministers. The functions of both Acolytes and Lectors are carried out by Priests or Deacons when there are no Acolytes or Lectors present and, as such, those functions are part of the

---

6 See GIRM 171–86.
7 See Paul VI, Apostolic Letter *Ministeria quaedam*, *Acta Apostolicae Sedis*, 64 (1972) 532; *Catechism of the Catholic Church*, 903.
8 The alb is the long, full-length, white or off-white garment that Deacons and concelebrating Priests wear under their stole.

ministry of Priests and Deacons, who are the ordinary ministers of the Word and of Holy Communion.

When no Deacon is present, Lectors may carry the *Book of the Gospels* to the altar, walking with the other ministers in front of the Priest. If there is no singing at the beginning of Mass and the entrance antiphon is not recited by the faithful, the Lector may read the antiphon. During the Liturgy of the Word, Lectors proclaim the readings that precede the Gospel from the ambo and they may proclaim the responsorial Psalm if it is not sung. If there is no Deacon present, Lectors may announce the intentions of the Prayer of the Faithful. If there is no singing at Communion and the Communion antiphon is not recited by the faithful, the Lector may read the antiphon.[9]

Acolytes may carry the cross in the procession to and from the altar. They may assist the Priest or Deacon in various ways during Mass. If there is no Deacon present, they place the corporal,[10] the purificators,[11] the chalice, the pall[12] and the missal on the altar after the Prayer of the Faithful. The Acolyte may assist the Priest in bringing the gifts to the altar. If incense is used, he presents the

---

9 See GIRM 48, 87, 194–8.
10 The corporal is the square, white, linen cloth that is put on the altar during the celebration of Mass before the bread and wine are placed upon it.
11 The purificator is a small, white, linen cloth used for purifying the chalice and the containers for the hosts after Holy Communion.
12 The pall is the small square of cardboard covered in linen that is placed on top of the chalice to ensure that the precious Blood remains uncontaminated.

thurible to the Priest and, after the Priest has incensed the gifts, the cross and the altar, he incenses the Priest and the people. If necessary, they assist in the distribution of Holy Communion and in the purification of the sacred vessels afterwards.[13]

Extraordinary Ministers of the Word and of Holy Communion

As part of the reform of the liturgy after Vatican II, lay people who were not instituted as Acolytes or Lectors were permitted to carry out the functions of Acolytes or Lectors on a temporary basis. We have already noted that the functions of both Acolytes and Lectors are part of the ministry of Priests and Deacons, who are the ordinary ministers of the Word and of Holy Communion. When lay people carry out the functions of Acolytes on a temporary basis, they are known as Extraordinary Ministers of Holy Communion. When lay people carry out the functions of Lectors on a temporary basis, they are known as Extraordinary Ministers of the Word. The ministries of Acolytes and/or Lectors are permanent (without a fixed term) and universal (they may exercise their ministry in any parish or diocese). The ministries of Extraordinary Ministers of the Word and of Extraordinary Ministers of Holy Communion, on the other hand, are for a fixed term and limited to their local parish.

------

13 See GIRM 187–93.

According to the *General Instruction on the Roman Missal* (100–1):

> In the absence of an instituted acolyte, lay ministers may be deputed to serve at the altar and assist the Priest and the Deacon; they may carry the cross, the candles, the thurible, the bread, the wine and the water, and they may also be deputed to distribute Holy Communion as extraordinary ministers. In the absence of an instituted Lector, other laypersons may be commissioned to proclaim the readings from Sacred Scripture. They should be truly suited to perform this function and should receive careful preparation, so that the faithful by listening to the readings from the sacred texts may develop in their hearts a warm and living love for Sacred Scripture.

By the end of the 1980s, liturgical ministry by lay people had become common and was widely accepted. In his apostolic exhortation on the vocation and ministry of the lay faithful, *Christifideles laici* (1989), Pope John Paul II said that parish priests should entrust to lay people those roles that do not require 'the character of orders' (23). The *Catechism of the Catholic Church* (1992) recognised (910) that:

> The laity can ... cooperate with their pastors in the service of the ecclesial community ... through the exercise of different kinds of ministries according to the grace and charisms which the Lord has been pleased to bestow on them.

During the 1990s, however, it became necessary to clarify the roles and functions that were reserved for ordained ministers and the roles and functions in which lay collaboration was possible. The 1997 instruction on the collaboration of the non-ordained faithful in the sacred ministry of Priest, *Ecclesia de mysterio*,[14] insisted that:

> It is necessary that all who are in any way involved in this collaboration exercise particular care to safeguard the nature and mission of sacred ministry and the vocation and secular character of the lay faithful.

The instruction 'noted with great satisfaction' that the collaboration of the non-ordained faithful in the pastoral ministry of the clergy had 'developed in a very positive fashion' in many places. It insisted, however, that collaboration with ordained ministers did not mean that lay people could always 'substitute for' those ministers. The homily during Mass, for example, may only be given by an ordained minister. Recognising that the distribution of Holy Communion by lay people was always 'supplementary and extraordinary', the instruction said that:

> Extraordinary ministers may distribute Holy Communion at Eucharistic celebrations only when there are no ordained ministers present or when those ordained ministers present at a liturgical celebration are truly unable to distribute Holy Communion.

---

14 See http://www.vatican.va/roman_curia/pontifical_councils/laity/documents/rc_con_interdic_doc_15081997_en.html.

Altar Servers

We have already noted that, in the absence of an instituted Acolyte, lay ministers may be deputed to serve at the altar, to carry the cross or the candles, to assist the Priest or Deacon by carrying things to and from the altar and to distribute Holy Communion as Extraordinary Ministers. When this role is carried out by those who have not yet been confirmed, they do not distribute Holy Communion and they are usually known as Altar Servers. Traditionally, only boys could be Altar Servers, but canon 230 of the 1983 *Code of Canon Law* allowed for female Altar Servers if the local Bishop permitted it.

Singers and Musicians

The *General Instruction on the Roman Missal* recognises that the choir exercises its own liturgical role. It should ensure that, in keeping with the different types of chants, the parts proper to the choir are properly carried out and that the active participation of the faithful is fostered through the singing. There should be a cantor or a choir director to lead and sustain the people's singing. When there is no choir, it is up to the cantor to lead the different chants, with the people actively taking part.[15]

During the entrance procession, the singing may be done either alternately by the choir and the people, alternately by the cantor and the people, entirely by the people or by the choir alone. The '*Kyrie eleison*' is ordinarily sung by the entire congregation, the choir or cantor having a part in it. If it is sung, the 'Gloria' is begun either by the Priest

---

15 See GIRM 103–4.

or, if appropriate, by a cantor or by the choir. It is sung either by everyone together, by the people alternately with the choir or by the choir alone. It is preferable that the responsorial Psalm be sung, at least as far as the people's response is concerned. The psalmist, or the cantor of the Psalm, should sing the verses of the Psalm from the ambo or another suitable place. The Gospel Acclamation, which is led by the choir or a cantor, is sung by all, being repeated if this is appropriate. The verse, however, is sung either by the choir or by the cantor. If it is sung, the Creed is begun either by the Priest or, if appropriate, by a cantor or by the choir. It is sung either by everyone together or by the people alternately with the choir. It should not be sung by the choir alone. As a rule, the Lamb of God should be sung by the choir or cantor with the congregation responding. The communion chant accompanies the distribution of Holy Communion and its purpose is to express the communicants' union in spirit by means of the unity of their voices, to show joy of heart and to highlight more clearly the 'communitarian' nature of the procession to receive Communion.[16]

Other Roles

There are a number of other liturgical roles. The sacristan is responsible for carefully arranging the liturgical books, the vestments and the other things necessary for the celebration of Mass. When it is appropriate, a commentator may provide the faithful with brief explanations or commentaries with the purpose of

---

16 See GIRM 48, 53, 61–2, 68, 83, 86.

introducing them to the celebration and preparing them to understand it better. Those who assist in taking up and in counting the collection, and those who meet the faithful at the entrance to the church and direct them to an appropriate place, also make an important contribution to the liturgy of the Mass.[17]

Coordinating the Preparation of the Liturgy

Each celebration of Mass should be prepared in accordance with the Missal and the other liturgical books under the overall direction of the one who has pastoral responsibility for the church where it takes place. There should be harmony and diligence among all those involved, and the ministry and particular competence of each one should be respected. The Priest who presides at the celebration, however, always retains the right of arranging those things that are his own responsibility.[18]

---

17 See GIRM 105.
18 See GIRM 111.

CHAPTER 4
THE PHYSICAL
ENVIRONMENT
OF THE MASS

This chapter describes the physical environment in which the Mass is normally celebrated, the way in which the different liturgical seasons are reflected in each celebration of the Mass and the significance of the different liturgical colours and postures.

The Physical Arrangement of the Church
The area where the Liturgy of the Word and the Liturgy of the Eucharist are normally celebrated in a church is known as the **sanctuary**. This area is marked off from the body of the church by a particular structure and ornamentation or by being somewhat elevated. Located centrally so that the attention of the people naturally turns to it, the **altar** represents Christ, the living stone around whom God's people are built into a spiritual house (see 1 Peter 2:4). Any floral decoration of the altar should be done with moderation and flowers should be placed around, rather than on, the altar. A **crucifix**, clearly visible to the assembled congregation, is to be placed on or near the altar. The readings are proclaimed at the **ambo**, which is located in such a way that the attention of the people naturally turns to it during the Liturgy of the Word. The **chair** from which the principal

celebrant presides over the assembled congregation is normally located centrally behind the altar, but it may be located elsewhere if the tabernacle is in that position or if the distance from the congregation would be too great.[1]

The **congregation** should be able to participate 'visually and spiritually' in the Mass and to be able to hear what is said 'without difficulty'. As well as helping it to exercise its role easily and conveniently, the location of the **choir** should make it clear that the choir members are part of the assembled congregation and should allow each choir member to participate fully in the sacramental celebration. The **organ** and the other **musical instruments** used should be in a position where they can be heard with ease by all and where they can sustain the singing of both the choir and the congregation.[2]

The Blessed Sacrament of the Eucharist should be reserved in a **tabernacle** that is in a prominent and readily visible place, either in the sanctuary or in some suitable chapel. An oil or wax lamp should be kept lighting to indicate the presence of the Blessed Sacrament.[3]

The Liturgical Seasons
During the course of the liturgical year, the Church invites us to 're-live' the different stages of the life of Christ from the period looking forward to his coming during Advent, his birth during Christmas, the mystery of

---

1 See GIRM 295, 298–9, 305, 308–10.
2 See GIRM 311–13.
3 See GIRM 314–16.

Christ's life during Ordinary Time and his death, resurrection and ascension during Lent and Easter.[4]

While the calendar year begins on 1 January each year, the liturgical year begins on the fourth Sunday before Christmas with **Advent** (from the Latin *'adventus'*, meaning 'arrival' or 'coming'), a time of preparation for the celebration of the birth of Our Lord at Christmas. The readings at Mass during the first part of Advent (until 17 December) invite us to prepare for Christ's return in glory at the end of time. In order that the full joy of the birth of the Lord is not celebrated prematurely, the use of flowers to decorate the altar and the use of musical instruments to sustain singing should be moderated during Advent.[5]

In many churches, the period of waiting for the celebration of Christ's coming is marked by an Advent Wreath: a garland of evergreens with four candles on its perimeter, three violet and one rose. On the first Sunday of Advent, one of the violet candles is lit. A second violet candle is lit on the second Sunday. The rose candle and the two violet candles are lit on the third Sunday of Advent, known as Gaudete ('Rejoice') Sunday. All four candles are lit on the fourth Sunday. Sometimes there is also a white candle in the centre and, if so, all five candles are lit during Mass throughout the Christmas season.

---

4 In Ireland, Veritas publishes a liturgical calendar each year and the dates of the different liturgical seasons, guidelines for celebrating Mass each day and the specified readings for Mass may be found there.
5 See GIRM 305, 313.

The period of **Christmas** begins at the end of Advent, on Christmas Eve, and it continues through Epiphany until the feast of the Baptism of Our Lord. It is marked by the joyful celebration of the birth of Christ.

From ancient times, there have been representations of the **Christmas crib** in churches during the Christmas season. The *Directory on Popular Piety and the Liturgy* (2001)[6] recommends that the image of the child Jesus be placed 'in a crib in the church or somewhere nearby' after Midnight Mass.[7] The figures of the Magi are added to the crib for the feast of Epiphany.

Ordinary Time begins on the Monday after the feast of the Baptism of Our Lord. There are thirty-three or thirty-four[8] numbered weeks of Ordinary Time and, since it is the Sunday on which the second week of Ordinary Time begins, the Sunday following the Baptism of the Lord is the Sunday of the Second Week of Ordinary Time. Depending on the date of Easter,[9] there are between three and eight weeks of Ordinary Time before Lent. The days of Ordinary Time, and especially the Sundays, are devoted to the mystery of Christ in all its aspects and, during this period between Christmas and Lent, the readings during Mass focus on the early life of Jesus and on the beginning of his public ministry.

---

6 See http://www.vatican.va/roman_curia/congregations/ccdds/
documents/rc_con_ccdds_doc_20020513_vers-direttorio_en.html.
7 See the *Directory on Popular Piety and the Liturgy*, 104, 111.
8 Depending on whether there are fifty-two or fifty-three weeks in the year.
9 The canonical rule is that Easter is the first Sunday after the fourteenth day of the lunar month that begins on or after 21 March.

The period of preparation for Easter, known as **Lent**, coincides with the final period of preparation for Adult Baptism at the Easter Vigil. It recalls the forty years during which the Israelites wandered in the wilderness before entering the Promised Land and the forty days that Jesus spent in the wilderness following his Baptism in the Jordan. Beginning on Ash Wednesday and ending on Holy Saturday, and excluding the six Sundays, there are forty days of Lent. In keeping with its sombre and penitential mood, the 'Gloria' is not sung during Lent and the 'Alleluia' before the Gospel is replaced with a different chant. The mood of Lent lightens somewhat on the fourth Sunday, known as Laetare ('Be Joyful')[10] Sunday. The final week of Lent, which begins on Passion (Palm) Sunday, is known as Holy Week. It ends with the Easter Triduum, the three-day celebration of Holy Thursday, Good Friday and Holy Saturday. Apart from Laetare Sunday, Solemnities and Feasts, it is forbidden to decorate the altar with flowers during Lent and musical instruments should be used only to support the singing.[11]

Easter begins with the celebration of the Easter Vigil, the most important Mass of the liturgical year, which is celebrated during the hours of darkness between sunset on Holy Saturday and sunrise on Easter Sunday. After the Paschal candle has been lit from the Easter fire and welcomed with the proclamation, 'The Light of Christ', the Priest, Deacon or cantor sings the *Exsultet* or Easter Proclamation. The 'Alleluia' before the Gospel is sung for the first time since the beginning of Lent and it is a

---

10 The first words (in Latin) of the Opening Prayer are '*Laetare, Jerusalem*'.
11 See GIRM 305, 313.

significant feature of the liturgy throughout the fifty days of Easter, which include the feast of the Ascension and end with the feast of Pentecost (literally the 'fiftieth' day).

Ordinary Time begins on the Monday after Pentecost, the weeks resuming their numbering at the point that will make the final week before Advent the thirty-fourth week. There are between twenty-five and thirty-one weeks of Ordinary Time in the period between Pentecost and the beginning of a new liturgical year on the First Sunday of Advent. The Sunday after Pentecost is Trinity Sunday and, in Ireland, the following Sunday is the solemnity of the Body and Blood of Christ. The final Sunday of Ordinary time, which is the Sunday of the thirty-fourth week, is the Solemnity of Our Lord Jesus Christ, Universal King.

The Liturgical Colours
According to the liturgical season (Lent and Advent, for example), or according to the particular feast being celebrated, particular colours are used for the vestments of Priests and Deacons, as well as for the hangings in the altar area: 'The purpose of a variety in the colour of the sacred vestments is to give effective expression even outwardly to the specific character of the mysteries of faith being celebrated and to a sense of Christian life's passage through the course of the liturgical year.'[12]

Up until the fourth century, the only liturgical colour used was **white**. This colour is associated with the divine glory of Jesus, our Lord. At his Transfiguration, the face of Jesus 'shone like the sun, and his garments became

---

12 GIRM 345.

white as light' (Mt 17:2). In the accounts of the resurrection of Jesus, the angels in or near the tomb are described as being dressed in white (see Mt 28:3; Mk 16:5) and the saints in heaven, who have come to share in his resurrection, are also described as being dressed in white (see Rev 3:4; 6:11; 7:9, 13; 19:13). Because of its association with the divine glory that Jesus shares with the Father, with the Spirit and with the resurrection, the colour white is used during the Christmas and Easter periods. It is also used on the feasts of Our Lord (other than his Passion), Trinity Sunday and, because of its association with the saints and angels in heaven, on the feasts of Our Lady, All Saints (1 November), saints like St John the Evangelist (27 December), who were not martyred, and the angels. It is, presumably because of our communion with the risen Lord, made possible through the institution of the Eucharist and of the ordained priesthood that white is used for the Evening Mass of the Lord's Supper on Holy Thursday and for ordination Masses. White is also worn on solemn feasts such as the Conversion of St Paul (25 January), the Chair of St Peter (22 February) and the birth of St John the Baptist (24 June). As an expression of hope in the resurrection of the dead, white vestments may be worn in Masses for the dead subject to the approval of the local episcopal conference.

In his *De sacro altaris mysterio* (1:65), which was written before he was elected as Pope in 1198, Innocent III noted that black was the liturgical colour for penitential and funeral liturgies, with *violaceus* (**violet or purple**) as an alternative. Today, violet or purple is the liturgical colour that is used during Advent and Lent, and this colour may also be used in Masses of a penitential character and in Masses for the dead.[13] When it is used during Advent, this colour should probably be interpreted as reflecting the mood of penitential preparation and expectation as we look forward to the celebration of the Incarnation and to Christ's return in glory. When it is used during Lent, it should probably be interpreted as reflecting the mood of penitential preparation and expectation as we look forward to renewing our baptismal promises and celebrating the resurrection during the Easter Vigil. Reflecting the more joyful mood of the third Sunday of Advent (Gaudete Sunday) and of the Fourth Sunday of Lent (Laetare Sunday), **rose-coloured** vestments may be used instead of violet in those places where it is customary. Violet (or, where it is customary, **black**, the traditional colour of mourning) is also used on All Souls' Day and in Masses for the dead.

Because of its association with the shedding of their blood by Jesus and by the martyrs, **red** is used for Passion (Palm) Sunday, for feasts of the Holy Cross and for the feasts of martyred saints, Apostles or Evangelists (including the Holy Innocents). Jesus told us that the grain of wheat only bears fruit if it falls into the ground and dies (see Jn 12:24) and Tertullian recognised that 'the blood of the martyrs is the seed of the Church'.[14] The appearance of what seemed like tongues of flame at the first Pentecost (see Acts 2:3) and John the Baptist's description of Jesus as the one who would baptise 'with the Holy Spirit and with fire' (Lk 3:16), seem to be

---

13 See GIRM 346–7.
14 Tertullian, *Apologeticus*, 50.

the reason that red is used for Pentecost and for Confirmation Masses. Red is also used in Masses for deceased Popes and Cardinals.

The colour **green** is used during so-called 'ordinary time' (outside Lent, Easter, Advent and Christmas), when the mystery of Christ's life is presented to us in the readings at Mass. It should probably be understood as an invitation to recognise that we have received a share in Christ's life through our Baptism and Confirmation, and that our communion in the mystery of Christ's life is strengthened every time we receive the Eucharist. The Psalms compare the shortness of human life to the withering of green grass (see Ps 37:2), but they also describe God as a shepherd who leads his flock to 'lie down in green pastures' (Ps 23:2). Jesus may have been making a prophecy about the destruction of the city soon after his death when he consoled the weeping women of Jerusalem with the words: 'For if they do this when the wood is green, what will happen when it is dry?' (Lk 23:31).

On more solemn days, festive vestments, those made from more precious materials, may be used even if they do not match the colour of the day.[15]

Posture During Mass[16]
The congregation stands, sits or kneels together and their common posture is both a sign of their unity as members of the Christian community, who have gathered for the sacred liturgy, and an expression of their

---

15 GIRM 346.
16 See Joseph Ratzinger, 'The Body in the Liturgy' in *The Spirit of the Liturgy* (San Francisco: Ignatius Press, 2000), pp. 171–224.

shared intention and spiritual attitude. The general norms for standing sitting and kneeling are outlined in what follows.[17] However, in the light of local culture and traditions, the postures to be adopted in each country are determined by the Conference of Bishops and 'the faithful should follow the directions which the Deacon, lay minister or Priest gives according to whatever is indicated in the Missal'.

The faithful normally **stand** from the beginning of the Entrance chant, or while the Priest approaches the altar, until the end of the Opening Prayer. They stand again for the 'Alleluia' chant before the Gospel and remain standing while the Gospel itself is proclaimed. They stand during the Profession of Faith and the Prayer of the Faithful. They stand again when the celebrant says, 'Pray, brethren, that our sacrifice may be acceptable to God the Almighty Father', before the Prayer over the Offerings and, apart from kneeling for the Consecration and kneeling or sitting during the silence after Communion, they remain standing until the end of Mass. Unlike an audience at a play, who take no active part in what they are watching, our standing posture during Mass reflects our active engagement in what is going on. We sit or kneel at certain points for a relatively short time. The angels are described as standing in God's presence, ready to do his bidding (see Lk 1:19), and we hope to join them after our resurrection from the dead (see 2 Cor 4:14; Jude 1:24; Rev 7:15). Our standing posture at Mass gives expression to our solidarity with the angels and with the saints.

---

17 See GIRM 42–3, 96.

The faithful normally **sit** 'while the readings before the Gospel and the responsorial Psalm are proclaimed and for the Homily and while the Preparation of the Gifts at the Offertory is taking place'. They may either sit or kneel while the period of sacred silence after Communion is being observed. At Bethany, Mary sat at the feet of Jesus, listening to his words (see Lk 10:39), and Jesus described those who sat around him, listening to his words in order to do the will of God as his brothers and sisters (see Mk 3:32-34).

The faithful normally **kneel** 'at the consecration, except when prevented on occasion by reasons of health, lack of space, the large number of people present or some other good reason. Those who do not kneel ought to make a profound bow when the priest genuflects after the consecration'. Unlike sitting or standing, kneeling implies adoration (see Isa 45:23; Mt 4:9; Acts 10:26). It is the proper posture to adopt before the One who 'humbled himself and became obedient unto death, even death on a cross', the One before whom 'every knee should bow, in heaven and on earth and under the earth' (Phil 2:8-10).

CHAPTER 5
UNDERSTANDING THE
TECHNICAL TERMS[1]

Some of the unusual words used to describe or to explain the Mass can alienate us from what is taking place and prevent us entering fully and actively into the process of transformation that takes place during Mass. What, for example, does the first Eucharistic Prayer mean when it says that we offer bread and wine to God 'in sacrifice'? In what sense are the bread and wine 'sacrificed'? What does the second Eucharistic Prayer mean when it says that the bread and wine 'become for us the body and blood of our Lord, Jesus Christ'? What kind of change is involved in 'transubstantiation'?

Although we cannot fully explain the mystery that takes place during Mass, we know that the Holy Spirit is guiding the Church into the fullness of the truth (see Jn 16:13) and that its teaching helps us to clarify what we believe about the Mass. This chapter outlines the way in which the Church has come to understand the relationship between the Mass and the self-sacrifice of Christ on Calvary, the way in which bread and wine become the Body and Blood of Christ, and the

---

1 See Leo C. Hay OFM, *Eucharist: A Thanksgiving Celebration* (Message of the Sacraments, 3A) (Wilmington, Delaware: Michael Glazier Inc., 1989).

relationship between the Eucharist and the Mystical Body of Christ.

The Mass is the Sacrament of Christ's Self-Sacrifice[2]

We have seen, in chapter one, that the words of Jesus in the Passover setting of his Last Supper associated his death with the sacrifice of the Paschal Lamb. God the Father did not spare his own Son (see Rom 8:32), who became 'our Paschal Lamb' (1 Cor 5:7), making atonement for our sins (see Rom 3:24-25) and reconciling us with God (see 2 Cor 5:19).

The word 'sacrifice' is generally used to describe something that is given up for the sake of something else that is considered more valuable or important. In a religious context, sacrifices often took the form of an animal or vegetable offering that was consecrated on the altar of some deity in order to restore or foster the goodwill of that deity. The offering was normally food of some kind and its consecration involved its partial or total destruction, usually by some combination of burning or killing or eating/drinking. Some part of the bread and wine offered in thanksgiving by Melchisedek (see Gen 14:18) was probably consumed as a sacrificial meal and, in Jewish communion sacrifices (see Deut 14:26), the flesh of the animal was normally eaten. It was forbidden to consume the animal's blood, which was identified with the divine gift of life (see Lev 17:14; Deut 12:16).

---

2 See Nicholas Lash, *His Presence in the World: A Study in Eucharistic Worship and Theology* (London: Sheed and Ward, 1968).

Since it involves the offering of bread and wine 'in sacrifice'[3] to the Father, offerings that are consecrated by becoming the Body and Blood of Christ before being consumed as a Holy Communion, the Eucharist is also a sacrifice. Unlike the sacrifice of the Paschal Lamb, both the Body and the Blood of Jesus are consumed, for it is both by eating his Body and by drinking his Blood that we become one Body in him and come to share in his divine life.

Some of the sixteenth-century Reformers argued that it was only on Calvary, rather than at the Last Supper, that Jesus offered himself as a sacrifice to God. They held that the Mass should not be identified with the 'once for all' (Heb 7:27) and unrepeatable sacrifice of Calvary. It was a commemoration of the sacrifice of Calvary or an offering of praise and thanksgiving, but not, as such, the sacrifice of Christ's life for the salvation of humanity. Distinguishing between the visible and repeatable sacrifice of the Mass and the invisible and 'once for all' sacrifice of Calvary, the Council of Trent insisted, nevertheless, that the sacrifice of Calvary was the sacrifice offered at every Mass. Its *Doctrine of the Most Holy Sacrifice of the Mass* (1562) said that Christ left a visible sacrifice to the Church, as the nature of humanity demanded. By means of this visible sacrifice, his bloody sacrifice on the cross 'would be represented, its memory perpetuated until the end of the world and its salutary power applied for the forgiveness of the sins which we daily commit'.

---

3 See Eucharistic Prayer I.

In this divine sacrifice, which is celebrated in the Mass, the same Christ who offered himself once in a bloody manner on the altar of the cross is contained and is offered in an unbloody manner.

The bread and wine that are offered in the Most Holy sacrifice of the Mass become the Body and Blood of Christ. As a result, the victim in this visible sacrifice is 'one and the same' as the victim of the sacrifice of Calvary. Trent put it this way: 'The same now offers through the ministry of Priests, who then offered himself on the cross; only the manner of offering is different.'

The manner of offering the sacrifice in the Mass differs from the manner in which the same sacrifice was offered on Calvary. In the Mass, Christ's 'once for all' self-sacrifice on Calvary is offered in a sacramental manner, using the sacred signs of bread and wine that Jesus himself gave us at the Last Supper. The Mass is not a repetition of Calvary, for Christ died only once. It is as though the time and space in which we now live were somehow collapsed so that his one sacrifice become truly present among us in our space and time. It is the same sacrifice made sacramentally present whenever and wherever we do what he commanded us in his memory. In this way, our offering of bread and wine becomes his sacrifice on Calvary and his sacrifice on Calvary can be offered in many different places and at different times. When we receive the Eucharist, our senses continue to see and to taste bread and wine, even though our faith assures us that we are receiving the Body and Blood of Christ. We believe that the Priest acts in the person of Christ and that, in and through him,

Christ's self-offering at the Last Supper and on Calvary is made present in our midst. We do not see or hear Christ, however, because the sacrifice is now offered in a sacramental manner. The actions and words of the Priest who acts in the person of Christ are a sacred sign or sacrament of the actions and words of Christ, which remain beyond the reach of our senses, but which are powerfully effective nonetheless. When the Priest, speaking in Christ's name, declares, 'This is my Body ... this is my Blood', the Body and Blood of the risen Christ really become present, but not to our senses. Christ's death on the cross and the draining of his Blood from his Body (see Jn 19:34) is also truly, but mysteriously, present. Christ's death on Calvary is not perceived by our senses, although it is represented by the physical separation of the host and the chalice. As Pope Paul VI put it in his *Profession of faith* (1963), the Mass is 'the sacrifice of Calvary rendered sacramentally present on our altars'. In his encyclical for Holy Thursday 2003, *Ecclesia de Eucharistia* (11), Pope John Paul II described the Eucharist as the sacramental re-presentation of Christ's saving death and resurrection.

At the Last Supper, Jesus interpreted his self-offering to the Father and his imminent death on the cross by instituting the Mass as 'the holy and perfect sacrifice'[4] of his Body and Blood and commanding us to eat and drink. Every time we celebrate this sacrament, we offer the same 'holy and living sacrifice' that Christ himself offered 'once for all', the sacrifice that has made peace

---

4 See Eucharistic Prayer I.

between us and God[5] and that brings salvation to the whole world.[6]

The Presence of Jesus and the Change of 'Substance'[7]

What did Jesus mean when he said, 'This is my body ... This is my blood'? When the Jews at Capernaum asked how he could give them his flesh to eat, Jesus insisted that his flesh is 'food indeed' and that his blood is 'drink indeed', and that the one who eats his flesh and drinks his blood 'abides' in him and he in them (see Jn 6:56). In the Eucharist, we receive the Body and Blood of Christ as food and drink in a way that brings about an abiding personal and spiritual encounter with Jesus. The early Christian writers all recognised that the bread and wine were converted into the flesh and blood of Christ. St Augustine, for example, distinguished between the bodily appearance of what was seen and the spiritual fruitfulness of what was understood to be present. In the eleventh century, Berengar of Tours denied that the Eucharist actually was the Body and Blood of Christ, claiming that it was only a sign pointing to that reality. Lanfranc of Bec insisted that it was not only a sign pointing to the reality of Christ's Body and Blood, but that, as a result of the consecration, the bread and wine are changed into the reality towards which they point. Rolando Bandinelli, who became Pope Alexander III, coined the word 'transubstantiation' to describe this

---

5 See Eucharistic Prayer III.
6 See Eucharistic Prayer IV.
7 See Joseph M. Powers SJ, *Eucharistic Theology* (New York: Herder and Herder, 1972); Raymond Moloney SJ, *Our Splendid Eucharist* (Dublin: Veritas, 2002).

change. The Fourth Lateran Council (1215) taught that Christ's 'body and blood are contained in the sacrament "under the appearances [*sub speciebus*]" of bread and wine after being "transubstantiated [*transubstantiates*]" as a result of divine power'.

St Thomas Aquinas pointed out that the change is not merely one of form, like the change from water to ice, but a change in the underlying reality or 'substance'. Before the consecration it was bread, but after the consecration it is no longer bread because it has become Christ's risen Body. Before the consecration it was wine, but after the consecration it is no longer wine because it has become the Blood of the risen Christ. It is precisely because the bread and wine have become Christ's Body and Blood that receiving the Eucharist brings us into personal and spiritual communion with the risen Christ. Also, because the Body and Blood of the risen Christ can never again be separated from one another as they were when he died on the cross, both the Body and Blood of the risen Christ are present in either species. We receive the risen Christ when we receive the host and chalice together or when we receive either separately. The *Decree on Communion under the Species of Bread Alone* (1415) of the Council of Constance affirmed that 'the body and blood of Christ are truly and integrally contained under the species of bread as well as under that of wine'. In 1551, Trent's *Decree on the Most Holy Eucharist* taught that the whole substance of the bread and wine becomes Christ and that the whole Christ (body, blood, full humanity and divinity) is 'truly, really and substantially contained under the appearances' of bread and wine. When the Body and Blood of Christ are consumed, Christ remains bodily and spiritually present for as long as the appearances of blood and wine remain. After that he is present spiritually, but he is no longer bodily present.

In his *Profession of Faith* (1963), Pope Paul VI outlined the meaning of the term 'transubstantiation' as follows:

> Thus in this sacrament Christ cannot become present otherwise than by the change of the whole substance of bread into his Body ... while only the properties of the bread ... which our senses perceive remain unchanged. This mysterious change is fittingly and properly named by the Church transubstantiation ... In the order of reality itself, independently of our mind, the bread and wine have ceased to exist after the consecration, so that it is the adorable Body and Blood of the Lord Jesus which from then on are really before us under the sacramental species of bread and wine, as the Lord willed it, in order to give Himself to us as food and to bind us together in the unity of his mystical body.

The Eucharistic Change and the Mystical Body of Christ[8]
When the bread and wine become the Body and Blood of the risen Christ, thanks to the invocation of the Holy Spirit and the words of consecration, the appearances of bread and wine remain unchanged. Because they still

---

8 See Paul Bernier SSS, *Eucharist: Celebrating its Rhythms in our Lives* (Notre Dame, Indiana: Ave Maria Press, 1993); Raniero Cantalamessa, *The Eucharist: Our Sanctification* (Collegeville: Liturgical Press, 1993); Jean-Marie R. Tillard, *Flesh of the Church, Flesh of Christ: At the Source of the Ecclesiology of Communion* (Collegeville: Liturgical Press, 2001).

look like bread and wine, his Body can be broken and eaten like bread and his Blood can be poured and drunk like wine. When the priest breaks the Eucharistic bread, Christ's Body, into a number of different pieces, each piece is not just a part of Christ's Body, something less than the whole. Canon 3 of Trent's *Doctrine on the Most Holy Eucharist* (1551) insists that 'the whole Christ is contained under each species and under each part of either species when separated'. Although truly present under the appearance of bread and wine, the risen Christ is unaffected when the Eucharistic bread is broken or the Eucharistic wine poured. Breaking the bread does not hurt or divide him, and if we were to chew the fragment that we receive, we would not be tearing his flesh or breaking his bones, even though it is his Body that we are eating. Christ is bodily present in the Eucharist and we must respect that presence, but he is not bodily present in exactly the same way as when he said, 'This is my Body ... This is my Blood'. In the Eucharist, he is present sacramentally, under the appearances of bread and wine, and only for as long as those appearances remain. His bodily presence in the Eucharist is 'visible' only to the eyes of faith. Any physical or chemical analysis of the Eucharist would reveal only the characteristics of the bread and wine, and there is no 'objective' or scientific way in which the presence of the risen Christ could be verified.

In the last section we noted that Pope Paul VI described Jesus as giving us the Eucharist 'to bind us together in the unity of his mystical body'. The term 'mystical body' is closely related to the change that takes place during the Eucharist, for it describes the mysterious and invisible unity and communion that those who receive the Eucharist share with one another and with the risen Christ. In a mysterious or 'mystical' way, he lives in us and we live in him when we receive the Body and Blood of the risen Lord. Just as branches united with the vine draw their nourishment from it, our sharing in his divine life is nourished when we eat his Body and drink his Blood. Although our external appearance remains unchanged and our human personalities retain their integrity and freedom, we are united with his life, death and resurrection when we allow him to nourish us with his Body and Blood. The unique calling and destiny of each person can only be fulfilled in Christ. It is only by becoming living members of his mystical Body that we can come to know the fullness of the finite gift of life that we received at our conception.

CHAPTER 6
LIVING THE MASS

How, in practice, do we go about making the Mass the centre of our everyday lives? How do we overcome the lack of connection between what we do elsewhere and what we do when we come to Mass? How do we allow our lives to be nourished more deeply by the Holy Communion that we have received?

Already in this book we have looked in some detail at what happens when we go to Mass and at how we should understand the Eucharist. In this chapter we will focus on the way each Mass affects and changes our lives, and on the way our daily lives find expression and fulfilment at Mass.

The Way the Mass Changes Us

The Body and Blood of Christ that we eat and drink at Mass look like bread and wine. They are not just ordinary food, however, and they do not become part of our bodies in the same way that what we eat and drink normally does. They are spiritual nourishment and rather than being transformed by us and becoming part of our bodies, they transform us, drawing us into a deeper spiritual communion in Christ's mystical Body, the Church. Respecting our unique and personal identity in the Body of Christ, the Eucharist helps us to discover or to deepen that identity, to grow towards full maturity as members of Christ's Body and to respond to the needs of that Body in different ways. Our Baptismal sharing in Christ's victory over sin and death is fortified, the Pentecost gift of the Spirit that we received at our Confirmation is renewed and our reconciliation with God in the sacrament of Penance is reaffirmed. The special sacramental graces of the Ordained, of the Married and of those who have received the Sacrament of the Sick are nourished and deepened. The charisms or special graces that individuals have received from the Holy Spirit for the good of the Church are given new vigour and direction. We are enabled to see with new eyes, to look beyond merely human possibilities and to love as Jesus loved us, without counting the cost. We look the same as we did before Mass and the situations to which we return are no different, but we have been changed and if we are prepared to allow that internal change to show itself, it can and will transform our lives. The Eucharist does not always change us in the way we want; sometimes it enables us to manage rather than overcome something that burdens us. God the Father knows the needs of his children, however, and, in giving us the Spirit-bearing Body and Blood of his Son, we know that we have received all that we need to grow to full maturity in Christ.

The Sacrament of Love
Jesus summed up the Ten Commandments in the commands to love God and to love our neighbour (see Lk 10:27) and he presented the institution of the

Eucharist as a commandment to love one another as he loved us (see Jn 13:34). Although its effect is probably different in the individual lives of all the many millions who receive it every day or every weekend, the Eucharist enables each one to love their neighbour as Jesus loved us, without counting the cost. Here it renews and strengthens the love of wife and husband, there it enables a parent to forgive the wrong done by a child. The hardened heart is softened, the weak limb is made whole, indifference thaws and long-dead feelings come to life once more. Burdens are lightened and what seemed humanly impossible can somehow now be faced. Like a door unlocked without our knowing it, we can still remain closed to the deep changes that the Eucharist brings about in our hearts if we do not recognise and respond to its transforming power. With God, nothing is impossible (see Lk 1:37) and, if we pay attention, we will discover the many subtle and extraordinary ways in which Jesus has given us a new and unexpected share in his unconditional love. As each discovery of this kind becomes a new motive for thanking and praising God, the thanksgiving (*eucharistia*) of our last Eucharist is extended into our daily lives. We learn from personal experience that the same Jesus who was bodily present to us in the Eucharist remains actively present and engaged in all that we do, making his command to love as he loved a yoke that is easy and a burden that is light (see Mt 11:30). He has entered into Holy Communion with us, drawing us into the intimacy of the divine life he shares with the Father and with the Sanctifying Spirit, a life of love. And we have entered into Holy Communion with him, inviting him to share our daily lives, our hopes and our fears, our joys and our sorrows, filling them with his divine love.

Living in Holy Communion with the Self-Sacrifice of Jesus

When we live in Holy Communion with Jesus, his love reaches into all the corners of our lives, healing and renewing all our relationships, leaving nothing untouched. In us, his love reaches out to our spouses, our children, our parents, our relations, our neighbours, our friends and acquaintances, our colleagues and fellow-workers and everyone we meet. Thanks to his Holy Communion with us, he is present wherever we are: in our homes and on our streets; in all the factories, offices, shops and buildings where we work; in all the sports fields and gyms, cinemas and clubs, restaurants and pubs where we spend our free time. There is a difference between the bodily presence of Jesus in the Eucharist and the way in which he is spiritually present in our lives as a result of receiving Holy Communion, but these two forms of his presence are, nevertheless, closely related. His spiritual presence in our daily lives is nourished by and is the fruit of his bodily presence in Holy Communion. However, his spiritual presence in our lives is also directly connected to the sacrifice of Jesus that will be offered at our next Mass. Because of our spiritual communion with him, because he is spiritually present in all that we do and because we have become part of his mystical Body, the Church, our lives can no longer be regarded as separate from his. When the bread and wine become his Body and Blood at Mass and when his Body and Blood are offered in sacrifice to the Father, our lives, too, insofar as they are lived in communion with him, are also offered in sacrifice to the Father. We find that we are not just observers of what happens at Mass but, in a true sense, active participants. Just as Jesus gave his life in sacrifice for love of us, our communion with him enables us to offer our lives to the Father as a spiritual sacrifice for love of him:

> All the laity's works, prayers and apostolic undertakings, marital and family relationships, daily work, relaxation of mind and body, if they are accomplished in the Spirit – indeed even the hardships of life if patiently borne – all these become spiritual sacrifices acceptable to God through Jesus Christ (see 1 Pet 2:5), which, in the Eucharistic celebration, together with the sacrifice of the Lord's Body, are most fittingly offered to the Father.[1]

Jesus is like a living stone that was rejected by humanity but chosen by God to be the cornerstone of the spiritual household that is the Church (see Isa 28:16). Our Holy Communion with him aligns our lives with his, enabling us to make his priestly sacrifice our own:

> Come to him, to that living stone, rejected by humanity but in God's sight chosen and honoured; and like living stones be yourselves built into a spiritual household, to be a holy priesthood, to offer spiritual sacrifices acceptable to God through Jesus Christ. (1 Pet 2:4-5)

---

1 Vatican II, *Lumen gentium* 34.

The Eucharistic Rhythm of Our Lives

The Eucharist both enables and expresses our communion with Jesus. Each Mass brings a new and deeper communion with him that makes it possible for us to unite our spiritual sacrifices with his 'once for all' sacrifice on Calvary. These daily spiritual sacrifices, which are made possible by his love, find their full and proper expression when we offer them to our Father at Mass together with the sacrifice of his Body. As our reception of Holy Communion bears fruit in the spiritual self-giving of our daily lives, and as our daily spiritual self-giving in love finds its fullest expression when it is united with the sacrifice of his Body at Mass, a kind of Eucharistic rhythm is established. Our lives in communion with Christ flow out from the Mass and flow back into the Mass. It is both the source and summit of our Christian lives.

In his encyclical for Holy Thursday 2003, *Ecclesia de Eucharistia* (6), Pope John Paul II described the Church as drawing 'her life from Christ in the Eucharist' and as being both fed and enlightened as a result. Enlightened and nourished by the Eucharist, our communion with one another in Christ, and through him with the Father and the Holy Spirit, can be both recognised and fostered. Drawing its life from the Eucharist, our communion in Christ achieves its most sublime expression when we gather, as one, around the altar for the celebration of Mass.